Seasonal Scoff

A COMPANION RECIPE BOOK
TO SUPER SCOFF

"Four seasons fill the measure of the year . . ."

Keats.

Seasonal Scoff

with an Introduction by The Hon. Angus Ogilvy

A collection of

SEASONAL RECIPES

Illustrated by Judi Jennings

Favourite Recipes
*given by the friends and supporters of
The Warwickshire Association of Youth Clubs
by whom it is published*

First published November, 1977
Second Edition February 1979

© Warwickshire Association of Youth Clubs
63 Willes Road, Leamington Spa, Warwickshire
Telephone Leamington Spa 20278

ISBN 0 9501389 2 4

PHOTOSET IN TIMES AND PRINTED BY COVENTRY PRINTERS
CANLEY, COVENTRY

Made and Printed in England

CONTENTS

This collection of recipes follows Super Scoff and Super Vino and is sold in aid of the Warwickshire Association of Youth Clubs.

We are grateful to the many purchasers of Super Scoff, all over the world, and to date we have sold just over 50,000 books, with an additional 5,000 copies of Super Vino.

The encouragement we have received from those who have purchased Super Scoff has led us to produce this book.

Although deep freezing, and world airlines, allow us to use all foods at any time, we have made these recipes seasonal as many of us enjoy using fresh produce throughout the year.

Doris Butterworth.

The Editors of Seasonal Scoff wish to thank their many friends who have contributed to the book; without their help the sequel to Super Scoff could never have been written.

They also thank

> Judi Jennings for all the drawings and the re-designed cover.

> Dr. John Fauvel for his many hours of work on the index.

> Mr. Reginald Rudge and Mr. David Line in the Coventry Printers for their patience and professional help.

> Mrs. Alan Sweet for help with the typing.

THE WARWICKSHIRE ASSOCIATION
OF YOUTH CLUBS.

The symbols used in this book are

     (E) = Economic

     (S) = Simple

     (F) = Can be Deep Frozen

     (☆) = Extravagant

TELEPHONE
01-546 8833

THATCHED HOUSE LODGE
RICHMOND PARK
SURREY

*Once again the Warwickshire
Association of Youth Clubs have
produced an original recipe book. I am
pleased to commend this sequel to
Super Scoff, and I feel sure it will be
as useful and beneficial as its
predecessor.*

Angus Ogilvy

ANGUS OGILVY
PRESIDENT
NATIONAL ASSOCIATION OF YOUTH CLUBS

Spring

". . . Bare winter suddenly was changed to Spring."

Keats.

SPRING RECIPES

Starters

Main Courses

Puddings

Miscellaneous

[s] SPINACH SOUP

2 10 oz. cans of spinach puree

2 pts. of milk

Chicken stock cube

A little lemon juice

Put all ingredients into a pan with stock cube and a fair amount of salt. Bring to the boil and soup is then ready.

Serves 8 *Miss J. Varley, Leamington Spa*

ANCHOVY SOUFFLE WITH COD'S ROE SAUCE

Souffle:

1½ oz. butter

1 oz. flour

1½ gills milk

4 egg yolks

5 egg whites

1 small tin anchovies

Pepper

Cod's Roe Sauce:

1 jar Swedish cod's roe

¼ pt. double cream

¼ pt. bechamel sauce

Snipped chives

Prepare the souffle case and set on a baking tray.

Melt the butter and stir in the flour, add the milk, and stir until boiling. Cool slightly, and add the egg yolks one at a time. Sieve the anchovies and add to the mixture with a little of the juice from the tin. Season with pepper. Whip the egg whites until firm. Stir one tbspn. into the mixture to soften it, and then quickly fold in the remainder. Turn into prepared case and bake in a moderately hot oven, 350 - 375°f for 20 - 25 mins.

Make bechamel sauce using ¼ pt. flavoured milk, 1 oz. butter and 1 oz. flour. Whisk in the double cream. Finally add cod's roe to taste and snipped chives.

N.B. This recipe does not need salt added!

Serves 4 — 6 *Mrs. R. Curtis, Alvechurch*

4

⊛ CREAMED CRAB & MUSHROOM

1lb. flaked crabmeat
7 - 8 mushrooms, peeled
  and finely chopped
2 egg yolks
Salt, cayenne and chopped
  parsley

2 small onions
$\frac{1}{4}$ pt. milk
$\frac{1}{2}$ oz. butter
$\frac{1}{2}$ oz. flour

Make an onion sauce using the 2 onions and $\frac{1}{4}$ pt. of milk.
Season with salt, cayenne and chopped parsley. When sauce is
ready, stir in the crabmeat and the mushrooms. Simmer
together in a double saucepan for $\frac{1}{2}$ an hour. Remove from the
heat and stir in 2 beaten egg yolks. Fill shells, ramekins or a dish
with the mixture; sprinkle with buttered crumbs and bake or
grill quickly for 5 - 6 mins. to brown.

Serves 6   *Mrs. E. H. Lee, Warwick*

⑤ ICED WATERCRESS & SHRIMP SOUP

1 standard bunch of picked
  and washed watercress
3 oz. shelled shrimps (or
  prawns)

1 carton (5 fl. oz.) soured
cream
$7\frac{1}{2}$ fl. oz. milk
Salt and black pepper to
  taste

Put the watercress (with stalks) into your blender with the
soured cream and milk. Switch on fast for one minute and then
pour into a jug. Add the roughly chopped shrimps, taste and
correct seasoning. Add 4 ice cubes about 15 mins. before
serving.

Serves 4 - 6

|☆| ## SMOKED SALMON PATE

½ lb. smoked salmon pieces
  - minced or finely chopped
2 oz. butter
1 tbspn. saladin oil

2 tbspns. lemon juice
4 tbspns. double cream
cayenne pepper

Cream oil and butter, beat in smoked salmon and then the remaining ingredients.

Serves 6   *The Hon. Mrs. Smith Ryland, Sherbourne*

|F| |☆| ## SMOKED SALMON AND ASPARAGUS QUICHE

8 oz. shortcrust pastry
7 oz. Philadelphia cheese
4 oz. smoked salmon bits
2 eggs and 2 extra yolks
¼ pt. double cream

16 asparagus spears
  blanched for 5 mins.
  in boiling water
Salt, pepper, paprika
Parmesan cheese

Roll out pastry and line a 10″ flan case. Cream the cheese and mix with the beaten eggs. Cream, season well with salt, pepper and paprika. Chop the smoked salmon into small pieces and place on the pastry base. Pour over the cheese mixture and arrange the asparagus spears to form a star pattern, sprinkle with Parmesan and bake 35 - 40 mins. in moderate oven 375° Reg.5.

Serves 8   *Mrs. H. Lambert, Church House*
                              Welford upon Avon

(E) CHICKEN PANCAKES

4oz. flour	1 egg
Pinch of salt	$\frac{1}{2}$ pt. milk

Filling:

2 chicken breasts or remains of chicken	Salt, pepper
1 medium onion	1 tspn. fine herbs
2 pieces streaky bacon	$\frac{1}{2}$ chicken stock cube
1 tbspn cornflour	French bread
8 fl. oz. tomato juice	Tossed green salad

Fry bacon, remove from pan and cut into small pieces. Chop and fry the onion for 5 mins. in bacon fat. Chop or coarsely mince the chicken and add to onion and fry gently for 5 mins. Mix the cornflour with a little tomato juice and add with all the other ingredients together. Bring to the boil and simmer for 20 mins.

Blend the pancake ingredients together. Heat a nob of lard or butter in a 7" frying pan. Pour in just enough batter to cover the base, lifting the pan as you do so to ensure a thin layer. Cook quickly until golden underneath. Turn and cook the other side. Keep in warm oven and make seven more pancakes, putting a piece of greaseproof paper between each pancake to prevent it sticking.

Fill each pancake with the heated mixture and serve with a tossed salad and crusty bread.

Serves 4   *Mrs. Judi Jennings*

[E] [F] SMOKED MACKEREL PATE

2 smoked mackerel
$\frac{1}{2}$ lb. butter
$\frac{1}{4}$ - $\frac{1}{2}$ pt. of cream

Juice of a lemon
Salt and black pepper

Skin and bone the mackerel. Melt butter gently, beat or liquidise with the mackerel, then add the cream, lemon juice and seasoning.

Serves 6 — 8 *Mrs. F. Ashworth, Barford*

TRUITES EN GELEE

1 trout per person
White wine
White vinegar
Sherry
Black peppercorns

1 sliced onion
1 oz. aspic crystals
2 lemons
Chopped chives and parsley

Make court bouillon with equal parts of water and white wine, 2 tbspns. vinegar, sliced onion and peppercorns. Boil for a few minutes. Clean and trim trout, leaving heads on. Poach in court bouillon for 10 mins. (or according to size). Remove, allow to cool and skin. Boil remaining liquid in pan rapidly to reduce and strain. Dissolve aspic crystals and make up to 1pt. using liquid, juice of lemons and sherry (it is important that this jelly should have a good lemony flavour). Coat fish arranged on dish when on point of setting and sprinkle liberally with chopped chives and parsley. (1pt. of aspic will coat 6 - 8 fish.)

Mrs. P. Arkwright, Swalcliffe

Ⓢ Ⓕ   ## SPANISH PATE

Quantities are enough for two dishes, one for eating now and one for freezing. Serve with French or wholemeal bread

12 thin rashers unsmoked streaky bacon	Tbspn. chopped parsley
	Tbspn. chives marjoram
½ lb. chicken or other poultry livers	2 level tspns. salt
	Black pepper
1 lb. pig's liver	¾ level tspn. ground mace
½ lb. chuck steak	1 egg
1¼ lb. belly of pork	2½ oz. dry sherry
¾ lb. fat bacon	4 tbspns. brandy
3 cloves garlic crushed	3 oz. stuffed manzanilla olives

Line two 1½ - 2 pt. loaf tins with the streaky bacon rashers. Trim waste skin, etc., from the rest of the meat and mince it. (Alternatively you could use an electric chopper). Mix well with remaining ingredients. Fry a spoonful, taste, and add more seasoning if necessary. Fill the loaf tins and stand in a roasting tin with an inch of boiling water. Bake for 1¾ hours at 300°.

Each dish serves 8   *Mrs. A. Bennett, Warwick*

(F)

LAMBS' SWEETBREADS
and ARTICHOKE HEARTS

8 lambs' sweetbreads

8 artichoke hearts*

1 oz. butter

1 oz. grated Parmesan cheese

2 yolks of eggs

(*Tinned at this season)

2 tbspns. bechamel sauce

½ pt. good stock

2 or 3 slices of bacon

1 onion

1 carrot

Salt and pepper

Mixed herbs - parsley, thyme, bay leaf

Blanch and drain the sweetbreads.

Put the bacon - in 1" square pieces (roughly!) chopped onion, shredded carrot and herbs in a fire proof dish. Cover with stock, add seasoning, put sweetbreads on top. Cover with tin foil paper and put in oven number 5 for 30 mins. — but **do** baste frequently and add more stock if necessary. Strain the stock from the sweetbreads and place them on a warm dish to keep hot.

Put stock in saucepan, add bechamel sauce with egg yolks already beaten into it. Stir and cook gently.

Open artichoke tin and drain liquor.

Grease a shallow fire proof dish. Place artichokes on dish. Place sweetbreads carefully on top of hearts. Cover with sauce. Sprinkle liberally with Parmesan cheese. Dot with butter.

At this stage the dish can be covered and deep frozen.

Place covered dish in hot oven either to warm through from frozen or to heat up and uncover at last moment (with a quick dash under a hot grill to "bubble" the cheese).

It is economical of time to make 2 or 3 dishes of these and deep freeze the surplus ones.

Note: One 14 oz. can of artichoke hearts serves 5 persons i.e. 2 hearts each!

Serves 5 — 6   *Mrs. J. Butterworth, Coventry*

GUINEA FOWL

(F)

2 fresh long-legged guinea   6 oz. butter
  fowl   Salt and black pepper
2 medium sized onions   2 tbspns. water

Roast the guinea fowl in a covered roaster, placing 1 skinned whole onion and 1oz. butter inside each bird. Liberally spread remaining butter over each bird and sprinkle with salt and pepper. Put 2 tbspns. water in bottom of roaster and cook approx. 40 mins. in hot oven - 400°f. Remove and allow to cool slightly. When cool enough to handle remove meat from bone in large pieces and place in oven-proof casserole.

Sauce:
1 oz. butter   1 oz. flour   1 pt. stock

1 pint of stock made from pouring pint of water and 1 bottle red wine onto bones, giblets and juices from pan — boil hard for 1½ hours. Add 1 lb. glazed pickling onions and ½ lb. sliced mushrooms, sauted in lemon juice. Pour over the meat in casserole and heat through before serving. A little cream can be added if desired.

    This dish can be used for large numbers, useful in that it can be done in stages — freezing the cooked fowl and stock separately to assemble with the onion and mushroom when required.

Serves 6 — 8   *Mrs. P. Beney, Warwick*

BARBECUED TURKEY BREAST

1 turkey breast	2 tbspns. Worcester sauce
2 tbspns. butter or margarine	9 tbspns. ketchup
1 clove garlic	1 tbspn. sugar
3 tbspns. vinegar	1 tspn. sweet basil
1 tbspn. lemon juice	Salt, pepper to taste

Melt butter or margarine, add garlic and cook for 2 mins. Discard garlic. Add remaining ingredients and heat to boiling point. Brush turkey with sauce and place on a rack, skin side down, roast at 325° for 30 mins. basting often with sauce. Turn and roast for further 30 mins. until turkey is tender.

Serve with rice or mashed potatoes.

Serves 4 — 6   *Mrs. R. Jennings, Leamington Spa*

LAMBS' KIDNEYS

4 lambs' kidneys	2-4 tbspns. Port and
4 tbspns. butter	Armagnac
1-2 tspns. Dijon mustard	2-4 tbspns. Pâté Parfait
Salt and black pepper	1-2 tbspns. lemon juice

Skin kidneys and saute quickly in half the butter and allow to stiffen and brown while still remaining almost raw.

Dice kidneys, melt remaining butter in thick bottomed frying pan and add kidneys, mustard, salt and pepper. Stir well over high flame for 1-2 mins. before adding port. Sprinkle the kidneys with Armagnac and ignite, stir continuously until alcohol has disappeared.

Mash pâté with a fork until well blended. Stir into sauce and cook for further 1-2 mins. until kidneys are tender. Do not allow sauce to boil. Just before serving, stir in lemon juice. Serve with boiled new potatoes or rice.

Serves 2   *Mrs. P. Wartnaby, Leek Wootton*

ⓢ SWEET AND SOUR CHICKEN

1 chicken cut into pieces	1 cup tomato ketchup
1 onion	3 tbspns. Worcester sauce
2 tbspns. cooking oil	$1/2$ tbspn. prepared mustard
2 tbspns. vinegar	1 cup water
2 tbspns. brown sugar	$1/2$ cup chopped celery
$1/4$ cup lemon juice	seasoning

Brown the floured chicken pieces in oil and remove to a casserole. Fry onion, add rest of ingredients. Simmer for 1 min. Pour sauce over chicken and bake in moderate oven for 1 hour.

Serves 4 — 6 *Mrs. J. Butterworth, Coventry*

BOILED LAMB IN CAPER SAUCE

1 leg or shoulder of lamb	2oz. flour
1 onion chopped	1 - 2 tbspns. capers
1 carrot chopped	2 tbspns. cream
Bouquet garni	Salt and pepper
2 oz. butter	(Retain cooking stock)

Place lamb in large saucepan, cover with cold water and bring slowly to the boil.

Skim the water carefully, and add onion and carrot, bouquet garni, salt and pepper. Simmer very slowly until meat is just done (between 1 and 2 hours depending on size of joint). Remove meat and keep warm while making sauce.

Sauce: Melt butter in heavy pan, add flour and cook gently for 2 mins. stirring all the time. Gradually add $3/4$ pt. of strained lamb stock.

Stir until smooth, add capers and cream and check seasoning.

Good way of using New Zealand lamb.

Serves at least 6 *Mrs. P. Wartnaby, Leek Wootton*

(F) ## CHICKEN AND LEEK PIE

1 cooked chicken simmered in stock or court boullion	2 sticks celery
1 large onion	1 carrot
	Bouquet garni

Pastry:

8 oz. (250gm) flour	1 egg yolk
5 oz. (150gm) butter	Water

4 oz. (125gm) cooked tongue	2 tbspns. cream
6 medium leeks	2 tbspns. flour
2 tbspns. parsley	

Truss the chicken and place in a large pan. Half cover the bird with cold water. Bring to the boil and skim well and add all the vegetables left whole. Season. Cover the pan and simmer until the bird is tender, turning it over halfway through the cooking. Allow 1 hour for a roasting bird and at least 3 for a boiler. Allow to cool in the liquid. Reserve stock.

Carve the chicken, removing the skin, and remove all the flesh from the bones. Arrange this in a pie dish with the tongue also cut into neat pieces. Wash and trim the leeks and cut into pieces. Cook these briskly in boiling salted water 3 - 4 mins. Refresh under the cold tap and drain well. Add to the pie dish together with the parsley and seasoning. Blend the flour to just enough cold stock barely to cover the chicken etc., add the cream and pour over chicken in dish.

Make up the pastry. Place the flour on a board and make a well in the centre. Add the butter and the egg yolk and work up to a dough gradually drawing in the flour and adding a little water as necessary. Knead very well and leave to relax at least $\frac{1}{2}$ an hour. Roll out the pastry and cover the pie in the usual way. Decorate with pastry leaves. Brush with beaten egg. Leave in a cool place for 10 - 15 mins.

Bake for 10 - 15 mins. at Reg. 7, 425°f, then lower the heat to Reg. 4 - 5, 350 - 375°f and bake for a further 30 mins. Serve hot or cold.

Serves 8 — 10   *University of Warwick, Cookery Club*

CHICKEN SAUTE À LA CLAMART

1 3½ lb. chicken
2½ oz. butter
1 lb. shelled petit pois, fresh
   or thawed from frozen
1 head of lettuce
12 spring onions
2 oz. thick cut smoked
bacon diced small

Few tbspns. chicken stock if
   necessary
Salt, pepper
3 tspns. sugar
1 tspn. potato flour slaked
   with water

Joint chicken into four or more portions. Melt butter in a fireproof casserole (not iron or aluminium), place chicken joints in one layer and fry very gently until sealed, do not brown. Turn and seal other sides. Add spring onions and bacon, season with salt and pepper (a little tarragon or summer savory is good too), cover with chicken carcass if there is room and close tightly; place in a low 300° oven for ¾ - 1 hour or until nearly cooked. Remove the carcass, add peas, chopped lettuce and sugar and a little chicken stock if necessary though the chicken will have probably produced enough juice. Stir well together, cover and cook at a gentle simmer or in a 350° oven for 25 - 30 mins. Remove chicken joints to serving dish. Thicken peas if desired with a litttle potato flour and water or cream, pour over joints, serve all together in the casserole.

Serves 8 — 10   *Nicola Cox, Farthinghoe.*
                                      Fine Wine and Food Ltd.

Ⓢ # ROASTED BABY LAMB WITH PROVENCE HERBS

Take a piece of loin or saddle of lamb and let it marinate for a few hours in a mixture of the following herbs: thyme, fennel, sage, basil, rosemary and two or three cloves of garlic with salt and pepper.

Then take the herb impregnated lamb, smear it all over with butter and roast it in a hot oven allowing 20 mins. to the lb.

When it is cooked, remove it from the oven and let it stand in a warm place for 10 mins.

While it stands, add to the juices at the bottom of the roasting pan (having drained off the fat) a tablespoon of brandy with a little stock and a walnut of butter.

Mix together and pass through a sieve to remove the bits of herbs.

Serves 6 — 8   *Mrs. D. Aylett, Balscott*

SWEETBREADS

2lbs. sweetbreads   Seasoning
½ lb. sliced mushrooms   Dash of Sherry (optional)
6 oz. cream   Butter-flour
1 chopped onion

Place sweetbreads in pan of cold water. Bring to the boil, drain at once and press between two plates. Remove any fat, membranes and skin. Soften onion in butter, add mushrooms and fry for a few minutes. Sprinkle with a little flour to absorb any remaining fat, add sherry, cream and season to taste. Put in the prepared sweetbreads and heat through. Serve at once with plain boiled rice.

Serves 2 — 4   *Mrs. J. M. Macnair, Ullenhall*

(s)

BARBEQUED LOIN OF BABY LAMB

1 rolled and trimmed loin of
   baby lamb

2 bay leaves

1 clove garlic

2 tbspns. olive oil

6 tbspns. dry white wine

Salt

Freshly ground black pepper

Crumble bay leaves, finely chop the garlic and crush. Mix all the ingredients together and fill the roll of lamb, tie securely. Leave overnight to marinate. To cook, place in a fairly hot oven - 375°f for 15 mins. then at 325°f for about ¾ hour. The lamb should be pink in the middle. Serve with petit pois and new potatoes.

Serves 6

LAMB PROVENCAL

1 leg of lamb to serve 6 - 8

1 large tin of anchovies

2 large onions finely
   chopped

2 - 3 tomatoes finely
   chopped

6 oz. mushrooms finely
   chopped

Wine glass of red wine

Vegetable stock

1 tbspn. of flour

Salt and pepper

Make cuts inside skin of lamb and insert ½ tin anchovies. Roast lamb in moderate oven. (Cover with foil until last 10 - 15 mins. of roasting.) Meanwhile prepare sauce:

Fry gently the onions, tomatoes, and mushrooms chopped in a little butter. Thicken to taste with the flour, vegetable stock and season. Add the other half of the anchovy fillets, chopped finely, with the wine glass of red wine.

Carve and arrange the lamb on a dish and pour sauce over. Sprinkle with a little very finely chopped parsley.

Serves 6 — 8   *Dame Margaret Shepherd, D.B.E.,*
Herefordshire

⬡ STUFFED SHOULDER OF VEAL

1 boned half shoulder of veal
(about 2lbs.)

6 oz. lean pork

6 oz. fatty pork, such as belly

6 oz. lean veal

1 small onion

1 clove garlic

$3/4$ oz. breadcrumbs

2 tbspns. chopped parsley

Salt and pepper

Fresh or dried sage

Fat or dripping

Trim off any excess fat and cut the shoulder of veal so that it lies in one flat piece.

To make the force meat, put the pork and the 6 oz. veal through the mincer. Chop the onion and garlic. Soak the breadcrumbs in a little milk. Add these to the meat, also the chopped parsley, salt and pepper and a little sage. Mix thoroughly together. Put this stuffing on the veal, roll it up and tie securely at $1/2$ inch intervals along the roll. Tie a string also from end to end to help to keep in the stuffing which tends to swell whilst cooking. Sprinkle with a little salt and pepper.

Place in a roasting tin with a very little fat or dripping, and roast in a hot oven (400°f, mark 6) for about $1\frac{1}{2}$ hours. The meat will give off during cooking some fat and juices which brown in the pan. If a little water is added from time to time as the juices evaporate, the liquid can be used to make a thin gravy.

Serves 6 *Mrs. J. Butterworth, Coventry*

⬡ VEAL ST. SIMON

4 veal escalopes

4 tbspns. Madeira or $1/2$
Marsala and $1/2$ dry Sherry

4-5 tomatoes, skinned,
de-seeded and chopped

4 oz. finely sliced mushrooms

4 oz. butter, preferably
clarified

$1/2$ pt. double cream

Salt, pepper, paprika

Trim the escalopes and beat them out very thin. Lay in a flat dish and spoon over the Madeira. Leave to marinate for 2-4 hours.

Melt the butter in a frying pan and when quite hot — or frothing if it is not clarified butter — lay the escalopes in it to cook quite quickly for about 4 mins., turning once. Take them from the pan and keep warm.

Add the tomatoes to the pan and cook them down to a pulp — this tomato puree helps to thicken the sauce which has no flour in it. Now add the finely sliced mushrooms and cook for 4-5 mins. longer. When the mushrooms are cooked, pour in the cream, season with salt, pepper and paprika and reduce over a brisk flame for about 3 mins, stirring in the pan juices and crusty bits. When you have a luxurious creamy sauce, return the escalopes to it for a few minutes to heat through and to allow the flavours to blend.

Serves 4   *Nicola Cox, Farthinghoe*
                                      Fine Wine and Food Ltd.

(E)   **MEAT LOAF**

1½ lbs. minced beef	2 large onions
6 oz. ham scraps and bacon scrap left-overs	1 tspn. mixed herbs
2 eggs	1 handful of parsley, finely chopped
1 tbspn. Worcester sauce	Salt and pepper
1 tbspn. Tomato ketchup	

Mince ham/bacon scraps and onions. Mix all ingredients together and press firmly into a loaf shape. Roll in seasoned wholemeal flour. Roast in dripping, basting occasionally, at 400°f for first ½ hour and then at 350° for last ½ hour. Serve with tomato sauce. (See recipe for Greek meat balls.)

This is equally good cold for picnics.

Serves 6 — 8   *Mrs. S. Edwards-Jones, Ullenhall*

NOISETTES OF LAMB
SAUCE PALOISE

1 best end of lamb   Salt, pepper   1 oz. butter

Sauce Paloise

2 egg yolks   1 tspn. chopped parsley
3 tbspns. white wine vinegar   4-6oz. butter
2 tbspns. dry white wine   Salt and pepper
2 tbspns. chopped shallot   1 tspn. mint, parsley or
2 tspns. chopped mint   chervil finely chopped

Bone out the lamb, sprinkle with salt, pepper and chopped herbs if you like. Roll up and tie 3-4 times with fine string, spread with butter and roast in a hot 425° oven for 30 mins. or according to size.

Sauce Paloise

Boil finely chopped herbs and shallot in wine and vinegar until reduced to about 1 tablespoonful. Gently melt all but 1oz. of butter in a saucepan. Beat egg yolks in a basin for about 1 minute until thick and sticky. Add 1 teaspoon of cold water to vinegar herb mixture and then beat into yolks gradually drop by drop. Place the bowl over a saucepan of hot water, add $\frac{1}{2}$ oz. of cold butter and stir until yolks thicken. Beat in remaining $\frac{1}{2}$ oz. of cold butter to stop cooking then beat in remaining melted butter drop by drop as for mayonnaise. Leave salty milky residue in pan. Season and beat in remaining chopped herbs. Keep warm over a saucepan of lukewarm water stood in a warm place for up to five hours. Any remaining sauce can be kept in fridge or freezer and beaten into soups and sauces.

Serves 4   *Nicola Cox, Farthinghoe*
                                      Fine Wine and Food Ltd.

GREEK STYLE MEAT BALLS

1lb. minced beef
1 onion, finely chopped
1 clove of garlic, finely chopped
1 pinch of mixed herbs
1 tbspn. Worcester sauce

Good handful of parsley, finely chopped
8 mint leaves, finely chopped
1 large egg
Salt and black pepper

Mix the above ingredients together, and press firmly into small balls, the size of a large walnut. Fry gently in dripping or oil until brown on the outside and cooked through — about 5 mins. each side.

Sauce:

1 14 oz. can of Italian tomatoes
1 large onion finely chopped
1 clove of garlic, finely chopped

1 tbspn. Worcester sauce
1 handful of parsley
1 tbspn. tomato ketchup
1 pinch mixed herbs
Black pepper and salt

Fry the onion and garlic gently for a few minutes, then add the rest of the ingredients except the parsley and simmer gently until the onion is cooked. Add the parsley and meat balls, and heat through. Serve with buttered spaghetti generously dusted with black pepper.

The meat balls on their own make an excellent addition to both hot and cold hors d'oeuvre.

Serves 2 — 4   *Mrs. S. Edwards-Jones, Ullenhall*

JAMBON A LA CREME

8 thick slices cooked ham
6 oz. button mushrooms
7 fl. oz. dry white wine
3-4 shallots
1 lb. tomatoes

2½ oz. butter
1½ oz. plain flour
8 fl. oz. cream
2 oz. Parmesan cheese
Salt and pepper

Trim mushrooms and slice thickly. Cook them in the wine until the wine has reduced to about 3 tbspns. Lift out mushrooms and set aside. Peel and finely chop the shallots — add to the wine and cook until the wine has evaporated. Skin tomatoes and chop roughly. In a separate pan, melt 2 oz. of the butter, stir in flour, and cook for 2 mins. Gradually add the cream to make a smooth sauce. Season, stir in shallots and chopped tomatoes and cook for 5 mins., stirring occasionally.

Arrange the ham in a fireporoof dish and sprinkle with the mushrooms. Pour over the sauce and dot with remaining butter. Cook for 30 mins. in oven at 400°f.

Serves 4 — 6 *Mrs. P. de Bunsen, Newbold Pacey*

LOIN OF PORK

2½ lb. loin of pork
½ lb. apple sauce
herbs

1 glass white wine or cider
seasoning

Bone and skin loin of pork. Remove surplus fat, season and rub with herbs inside. Roll and tie. Spread with thick apple sauce to which a few chopped herbs have been added. Put in roasting tin with the bones, dry white wine, or cider, salt and black pepper. Cook at 350°f basting frequently for about 1½ - 2 hours, adding a little water if neccessary.

Serves 6 *Mrs. J. Owen, Shipston-on-Stour*

(S) EASTER TART

1 lb. puff pastry
4 oz. ground almonds
3 oz. castor sugar
3 oz. melted butter
Grated rind of a lemon

1 egg
2 tbspns. cream
tbspn. rum (optional)
Icing sugar

Roll out pastry thinly into two rectangles equal sized. Mix next seven ingredients. Spread over one piece of pastry and cover with the other, closing edges firmly.

Bake at Mark 7 (425°f) for 20 mins. then Mark 4 (350°f) for 25-30 mins.

Dust with icing sugar. Serve warm with cream if liked.

Serves 6 — 8   *Mrs. H. Brown, University of Warwick*

(F) LEMON CHEESE CREAM

$\frac{1}{2}$ lb. Philadelphia cheese
3 tbspns. castor sugar
Few drops vanilla essence
Juice and rind of small lemon
2 egg yolks

$\frac{1}{2}$ oz. powdered gelatine
3 egg whites
$\frac{1}{2}$ pt. double cream
Plain chocolate for
   decoration

Blend together cream cheese, sugar, vanilla essence, add the lemon juice and finely grated rind. Then the beaten egg yolks and whisk all together. Put gelatine with two tablespoons of cold water into a cup and stand this in a saucepan with water coming half way up the cup and simmer gently until gelatine is dissolved then add to cheese mixture. Beat egg whites until stiff and fold in gently. Finally fold in whipped cream.

Pour or spoon into a shallow bowl and stand in 'fridge until set. Either leave in bowl or turn out onto a dish and decorate with coarsely grated plain chocolate.

Serves 7 — 8   *Mrs. J. Panks, Swalcliffe*

PINEAPPLE MERINGUE TORTE

1 lb. 4 oz. can
Pineapple pieces
4 egg whites
8 oz. castor sugar

½ pt. double cream
Pinch cream of tartar
4 oz. whole blanched
   almonds (or nibbed almonds)
Icing sugar

Several hours before required turn contents from can of pineapple into a saucepan and boil until juice is reduced almost entirely and the pineapple looks opaque. Cool. Whisk egg whites until stiff, add two tbspns. sugar and cream of tartar and whisk again until stiff. Fold in remainder of sugar and finely chopped nuts. Spread in two 8-9″ discs over non-stick baking paper placed on baking sheets. Dry in oven 300°f (Mark 2) for about 1¼ hours until almond meringue is crisp and paper peels away easily. Cool and store in airtight tin. Whip cream until thick enough to spread. Use about two thirds together with most of pineapple to sandwich meringue discs together. Place meringue on serving plate, dust with icing sugar. Pipe rest of cream around edge of torte in whirls, finish with reserved pineapple and place in refrigerator for several hours.

Countdown:

Almond layers and pineapple can be prepared in advance and assembled day of use.

Serves 6 — 8   *Mrs. J. Snook. Kenilworth*

(E) (S) RHUBARB GINGER CREAMS

An economical sweet when rhubarb is flourishing. Quite a good way of getting people who are not over-fond of rhubarb to eat it, as it really is delicious and not too obviously "rhubarby".

5 fl. oz. double cream	1 lb. rhubarb (pureed)
2 1/2 fl. oz. raspberry yoghurt	4 oz. ginger biscuits (crushed)

Whip cream until thick and place some in a piping bag to decorate dessert. Mix remainder with raspberry yoghurt and rhubarb puree. Arrange layers of this mixture alternately with crushed ginger biscuits in glass serving dishes. Top with piped cream and a few ginger crumbs. Keep in 'fridge until needed.

Serves 4 *Mrs. A. Gillitt, Leek Wootton*

(S) (F) RHUBARB AND GINGER ICE-CREAM

1 1/2 lbs. rhubarb	1/4 pt. double cream
6 oz. castor sugar	1/4 lb. crystalised ginger
1/4 pt. single cream	

Shake cut rhubarb over heat until juices appear, then add the sugar and cook. Puree, and add whipped cream. Fold in the ginger (cut into small pieces) and freeze immediately. Serve with ginger snaps and cream.

Serves 6 — 8 *Mrs. J. Winstanley, Barford*

SPARROW HALL CHEESE CAKE

Base:

3 oz. ginger nut biscuits   2 oz. butter

To make base melt butter and mix with crushed biscuits. Put in prepared dish and leave in 'fridge to set.

Filling:

½ lb. Philadelphia cheese   Few drops of vanilla
3 tbspns. sugar (less if   essence
   preferred)   ½ pt. double cream

Mix cream cheese, sugar and vanilla essence together until soft. Add cream to mixture and spoon onto ginger nut base and put in 'fridge to set. If liked before serving add one can of cherry pie filling on top or sliced ginger, or grapes or any kind of fruit. (1 tbspn. of lemon juice added to cherry pie filling improves the flavour).

Serves 6 — 8   *Mrs. J. Panks, Swalcliffe*

BROAD BEAN TIPS

Nip out the tips of your broad beans when they have reached the required height and wash well.

Cook in boiling salted water for about 5 mins.

Place a large knob of butter on top and toss well.

They are quite delicious, tasting rather like spinach.

Mrs. P. Beney, Warwick

(S)(E)(F)   ## CANNELLONI

2 tbspns. diced onion
1 lb. cooked minced meat or chicken
½ lb. cooked pureed spinach
1 tbspn. chopped parsley
A little grated nutmeg

Seasoning
Garlic (optional) chopped
1 tub plain yoghurt
1 egg
1 oz. butter

Sauce:

1 14 oz. tin tomatoes strained or 1 lb. skinned tomatoes
2 onions finely chopped

Seasoning, oregano
Cheese, Cheddar or Parmesan

Prepare Cannelloni as instructed on packet. Sweat onion in butter with garlic if used. Mix with other ingredients and bind with yoghurt and egg. Stuff or roll pasta with the meat mixture and put in oven-proof serving dish. Cover with sauce made as follows:—

Blend onions with tomatoes, add seasoning and cook gently with ½ tspn. sugar. Thin with a little tomato juice if necessary. Add herbs. Pour over Cannelloni. Sprinkle with grated cheese. Cook in moderate oven for about ½ hour.

Serves 8   *Mrs. J. Owen, Shipston-on-Stour*

ASPARAGUS CREAM

16 oz. frozen or fresh asparagus $\frac{1}{2}$ lemon
$\frac{1}{2}$ tspn. paprika   1 pt. of cream

Cook asparagus in salted water for 8 mins. Drain well. Chop off
the tips and reserve. Put the rest in the blender. Whip cream
with lemon until thick. Add the puree to cream, season and put
into glasses. Decorate with the tips of asparagus, dust with
paprika. Chill.

Serves 8

CREAMY CUCUMBER
AND MUSHROOMS

4 oz. almonds   3 tbspns. vegetable oil
1 large cucumber   Squeeze lemon juice
$\frac{1}{2}$ lb. button mushrooms $\frac{1}{2}$ lb. cream cheese
3 sprigs mint   Salt, pepper and nutmeg

To serve:

Cooked rice or creamy mashed potato   Lemon slices

Skin almonds by putting into small pan of cold water, boiling
for 2 mins. draining and rubbing off skins. Cut into shreds. Peel
and dice cucumber, wash and slice mushrooms. Saute almonds,
cucumber, mushrooms and mint in the oil for 5 mins. Add
lemon juice, cream cheese and seasoning. Heat through and
serve in a border of cooked rice or creamy mashed potatoes.
   Garnish with lemon slices.
   Other combinations are delicious. "Creamy courgettes and
mushrooms" are made in exactly the same way using $1\frac{1}{2}$ lbs.
courgettes instead of cucumber.

Serves 6   *Mrs. A. E. Mayne, Banbury*

ⓈⒺ CHEESY BACON STARTER

5 hard boiled eggs	$\frac{1}{2}$ pt. cheese sauce
5 slices bacon (streaky) fried	3 sliced tomatoes
1 large onion	Salt and pepper to taste

Boil the eggs, when cool, slice, fry bacon, remove from pan, cut in pieces, chop and fry onion.

Put equal portions onion and bacon in individual dishes.

Distribute egg slices equally over this mixture. Cover with cheese sauce. Decorate with tomatoes and sprinkled cheese.

Place under the grill until cheese melts.

Serve at once with Melba toast.

Can also be served in a big dish for supper.

Serves 4 — 6   *Mrs. R. Jennings, Leamington Spa*

ⓈⒺ LEEKS VINAIGRETTE

6-8 small leeks	2 tbspns. red wine vinegar
1$\frac{1}{2}$ oz. currants (soaked for one hour in boiling water)	4-5 tbspns. oil
	Salt and pepper
2 tbspns. fresh tomato pulp or 1 tbspn. tomato puree diluted with 1 tbspn. water.	Sugar to taste

Cook leeks in boiling salted water for 7-10 mins. Drain, refresh and drain again. Drain and dry the soaked currants. Put the tomato pulp into a basin with the vinegar, oil and seasoning, mix together. Sweeten to taste and add the currants. Split the leeks lengthwise and arrange in dish. Spoon dressing over the leeks and chill slightly.

Serve with hot rolls and butter.

Serves 4 — 6   *Mrs. M. Orton, Barford*

DOLMADES, WITH YOGHURT AND CUCUMBER SAUCE

30 young vine leaves (begged, borrowed or stolen from friend's prunings in April/May) (substitute cabbage leaves), or 1 can vine leaves

1 tbspn. tomato puree
1 pt. light stock
Juice of ½ lemon

Rice Stuffing

4 oz. rice
6 oz. minced meat
1 tbspn. chopped parsley

1 small clove garlic crushed
Oil, salt, pepper, lemon juice
1 shallot, chopped finely

If you are using fresh vine leaves boil in salted water 5 mins. Drain and spread out flat. Prepare rice stuffing.

Saute shallot in oil until transparent. Toss in meat, rice and cook for 10 mins., taking care not to burn. Add enough water to cover. Add parsley and lemon juice. Season. Simmer for 20 mins. or until rice is tender. Cool slightly.

Put a little stuffing on each leaf and roll up firmly. Place at the bottom of shallow ovenproof dish and cover with any odd bits of leaves. Pour over liquid and cook covered for 2 hours in slow oven, 300°f.

To serve hot: strain off liquid and reheat it adding a small carton of sour cream or yoghurt and pour over

To serve cold: allow to stand in liquid until cold. Drain and serve with carton of yoghurt or sour cream with chopped cucumber and chives and cayenne pepper to taste.

N.B. Do not be tempted to use old vine leaves as these are extremely tough and sinewy.

Serves 6 — 8   *Mrs. P. Beney, Warwick*

SEAFOOD CRUMBLE

[E]

2 lbs. fish — a mixture of cod, smoked haddock, prawns, scallops and mussels

4 hard-boiled eggs (chopped)
A little white wine (optional)

Crumble topping:

6 oz. flour
3 oz. butter

3 oz. grated cheese
(Parmesan and Cheddar mixed)

Sauce

1 chopped onion
1 pt. white sauce made from 1 $^1/_2$ oz. butter 1 $^1/_2$ oz. flour,

1 pt. reserved fish milk
Seasoning

Cook cod and haddock in milk. Cool, skin, bone and flake fish. Reserve milk for the white sauce. Soften the onion in butter, add the flour and milk from the fish and white wine if used, to make a pint of white sauce. Stir in all the fish, shellfish and eggs and pour into heat-proof dish. Sift together flour and seasoning into bowl, rub in the butter and cheese until mixture resembles breadcrumbs. Sprinkle on top of fish and bake in moderate oven for about $^1/_2$ hour until crumble mixture is crispy and golden. Depending on the type of fish used, this dish can be a very economical supper dish or a more glamorous buffet party affair.

Serves 6 *Mrs. J. M. Macnair, Ullenhall*

HOT EGG DISH

5 hard-boiled eggs $^1/_2$ pt. white sauce   2 onions softened

Take yolk out and slice egg whites. Place in bottom of dish and cover with onions. Cover with sauce and sieved egg yolks on top. Cook in oven for 20 mins.

Serves 4 *Miss J. Anthony, Sherbourne*

LEMON BARLEY WATER

2½ tbspns. pearl barley   3 lemons   3 pts. water

Just cover pearl barley with water. Bring to the boil. Strain through sieve retaining liquid. Add lemons, juice and rind and sugar to taste.

Cover with boilding water — boil for 15 mins.
Allow to cool and refrigerate.
Sieve before serving.

[E] [S]   **MUSHROOMS AND MINT**

Simple to make, cheap when mushrooms are plentiful — especially if you can pick some field mushrooms — Quantity for 6 people.

¾ lb. mushrooms
2 small onions
Large handful fresh mint
    leaves
3 cloves garlic

5 tbspns. olive oil
Juice of one lemon
Wine vinegar
Salt, black pepper

Into a saucepan pour the olive oil, the juice of a small lemon and about 1 tbspn. wine vinegar. Then put in a lot of freshly ground black pepper, a spoonful of salt, 3 cloves garlic (crushed or chopped very finely), roughly chopped mint leaves, sliced mushrooms and the onions peeled and cut into very thin rings. Mix all this with a spoon and put on a very low heat with the lid on for not more than 10 mins. Pour into a serving dish and cool in 'fridge. Serve with brown bread to mop up the juice.

Serves 6 — 8   *Mrs. A. Gillitt, Leek Wootton*

SAUCE FOR VEAL OR CHICKEN MARYLAND

4oz. butter   Juice of $\frac{1}{2}$ lemon

Chopped parsley $\frac{1}{2}$ pt. cream

Melt butter and parsley to sizzling point, add juice and cream and bring to boil, whisking all the time.

The Hon. Mrs. Smith Ryland, Sherbourne

Summer

"...for him the envious seasons roll,
Who bears eternal summer in his soul."

Oliver Wedell Holmes

SUMMER RECIPES

Starters

Main Courses

Puddings

Miscellaneous

(E)(S)   ## COURGETTE SOUFFLE

2 lbs. courgettes, cooked,   5 eggs, separated
  drained and mashed   6 oz. melted butter
8 oz. grated cheese (Gruyere,   Nutmeg and seasoning
  or Cheddar)

Mix together the courgettes, cheese, salt, pepper, nutmeg and
yolks and melted butter. Fold in the stiffly beaten egg whites.
Put in buttered dish and bake in medium oven (350°f) for about
$1/2$ hour. Sprinkle grated cheese on top.

Serves 6   *Mrs. B.W. Sutherland, Shipston-on-Stour*

TUNA FISH MOUSSE

Two 7 oz. tins tuna fish

White sauce made with:-

2 oz. butter, 2 oz. $1/4$ pt. home-made
flour $1/2$ pt. milk   mayonnaise (or Helmans)
3 eggs (separated)   2 hard-boiled eggs (chopped)
$1/4$ pt. double cream $1/2$ oz. gelatine softened in 3
2 oz. stuffed olives (roughly   tspns. water
  chopped)   Seasoning

Make up the white sauce and season well. Dissolve softened
gelatine in sauce while still hot. Beat in 3 yolks and allow to
cool. Flake fish and add to sauce with chopped hard-boiled
eggs, olives and mayonnaise. Whip cream and fold into mixture,
then whisk egg whites and fold them in. Pour into souffle dish
and allow to set. Decorate with stuffed olives, cucumber slices
and parsley.

Mrs. H. Lambert, Welford upon Avon

HADDOCK AND TUNA SOUFFLE

1 lb. fresh haddock (frozen
 will do)
7 oz. tin tuna fish
2 small cartons sour cream
2 tbspns. chopped chives

2 hard-boiled eggs
$\frac{1}{2}$ oz. gelatine, dissolved in $\frac{1}{2}$
 teacup white wine
Juice of $\frac{1}{2}$ a lemon
Salt and pepper

Poach haddock with a little milk, salt and pepper, in the oven, until tender at 300°f. Cool, and remove all bones and skin. Flake the fish, keeping all the juices.

Add the tinned tuna fish and mix with the chopped chives, chopped hard-boiled eggs, sour cream, freshly ground pepper, and salt to taste. Add the dissolved gelatine, mixing carefully. Taste and if required add the lemon juice. Set in the refrigerator.

This may be served in ramekins or a souffle dish and is particularly good with hot buttered toast.

Serves 4

(E)(S)   ## WATERCRESS SOUP

2 bunches watercress
1 clove garlic
1 bay leaf
$\frac{3}{4}$ lb. potatoes
1 onion

2 pts. chicken stock
$1\frac{1}{2}$ oz. butter
3 tspns. cream
Salt and pepper

Wash watercress, discard stalks and yellow leaves. Peel and thickly slice potatoes and onions. Put all in a large pan with pressed garlic, bay leaf, and stock and simmer until vegetables are tender. Remove bay leaf. Liquidise soup or press through sieve. Return to pan, re-heat and add butter and season well. Stir in cream just before serving.

Serves 6 — 8   *University of Warwick, Cookery Club*

AVOCADO SOUFFLE

2 avocados (not too ripe)   1 small onion
1 oz. butter   4 oz. bacon
1 oz. flour   4 eggs, separated
1/4 pt. milk   Salt and pepper
3 oz. Cheddar cheese

Soften the chopped onion in a little butter, add the finely minced bacon and fry a little longer. Melt the butter in a pan, add flour and mix well, gradually add milk stirring all the time and cook until the mixture forms a smooth ball. Beat in cheese, bacon and onion, then the yolks, one at a time. Continue beating until smooth and shiny. Whisk whites until stiff and fold into mixture with chopped avocado. Pour into buttered souffle dish and bake at 350°f for 30 mins. until golden.

Serves 6   *Mrs. J. M. Macnair, Ullenhall*

[E] [F] [☆] ## POTTED CRAB

2 lbs. crab (including shell)   Black pepper, mace, nutmeg
8 oz. slightly salted or   Cayenne pepper, salt
  unsalted butter   Lemon juice
Clarified butter to seal

Pick all meat from the crab, (keep flaky and creamy meat separate).

Season with salt, spices and lemon juice. Put the crab meats into a terrine, or individual remekins, in layers. Melt the butter and pour over the crab — there should be just enough to cover it. Leave to cool then cover with clarified butter, (about 1/4 ") and cover with foil when set to prevent cracking. This dish will freeze well and lobster may be used instead of crab.

Serves 6   *Mrs. W. Husselby, Fen End*

CUCUMBER AND
CHEESE MOUSSE

1 small cucumber	2 tbspns. white vinegar
6 oz. cream cheese	1 tbspn. castor sugar
1 tspn. onion juice	Pinch mace or coriander
¼ pt. boiling water or stock	¼ pt. cream, lightly whipped
½ oz. gelatine soaked in	watercress for garnish
3 tbspns. cold water	

Oil ring mould or individual ramekins. Dice cucumber finely or pulverise. Pour boiling water or stock onto soaked gelatine. Stir till dissolved then add to cheese. Mix cucumber with vinegar, sugar and spice. When cheese mixture is cold fold in cucumber and cream. Pour into mould. Refrigerate to set. Fill centre with watercress, and serve with brown bread and butter.

Serves 6 — 8   *Mrs. C. D. Collingwood, Coulsdon, Surrey*

(E)(S)   ## LEMON CHICKEN SOUP

1 pt. clear chicken stock, or bouillon stock cube and water	1 lemon
	Chopped chives
	Very thin lemon slices
3 eggs	Salt and pepper

Slightly heat stock, stirring constantly. Beat eggs, wash and dry lemon; grate rind into the eggs, extract the juice and gradually beat into the eggs. Stir in a little of the stock and beat until blended. Stir in the remaining stock and pour gently into the saucepan and stir over a low heat until soup thickens — do not allow to boil. Remove from heat, leave until cool and put in refrigerator. Season with salt and pepper, garnish with chopped chives and lemon slices. Serve very cold.

Serves 6   *Mrs. D. Aylett, Balscote*

HAM AND EGG MOUSSE

8 oz. cooked diced ham

4 oz. diced celery or
cucumber

4 hard-boiled eggs

2 tbspns. chopped chives

½ tspn. celery salt

Juice of half a lemon

½ oz. gelatine

¼ pt. chicken stock

4 tbspns. mayonnaise

4 oz. cream cheese

2 egg whites

Salt and pepper

Dissolve the gelatine in the stock and cool. In a large bowl put the diced ham, diced celery or cucumber, finely chopped hard-boiled eggs, and the chopped chives.

Sieve the cream cheese if necessary and add to the mixture with celery salt, lemon juice and mayonnaise. Mix well. Gently stir in the cooled gelatine, and season well. Whip the egg whites stiffly and fold in. Turn the mixture into a souffle dish and place in the 'fridge to set. Either turn out or serve in the dish.

Serves 6 — 8   *Ann Curtis*

AVOCADO BISQUE

2-3 ripe avocado pears

1 carton plain yoghurt

½ - ¾ pt. light jellied
chicken or veal stock

½ pt. of double cream

Salt, pepper, tobasco,

Worcester sauce

Remove skin and stones from the pears and rub through a nylon sieve with the yoghurt. Stir in the other ingredients and season well. Serve very cold.

If liked 2 oz. chopped prawns or 2 tablespoonsful finely chopped blanched or fresh chopped herbs could be added at the last moment.

Serves 6

E S F
COURGETTE SOUP

1 small onion, finely   ³/₄ pt. milk
  chopped   ³/₄ pt. stock
1¹/₂ lbs. courgettes
  (overgrown will do)

Sweat onions in a little butter. Add roughly chopped courgettes
and cover with milk and good stock. Cook gently until soft,
liquidise and serve hot or cold.

Serves 6   *Mrs. John Owen, Shipston-on-Stour*

☆

SMOKED SALMON, SCRAMBLED EGG
AND CREAMED SPINACH
6 eggs (scrambled)
6 slices smoked salmon
Creamed Spinach

2 lb. spinach   Pinch of Sugar
Pinch of grated nutmeg   Seasoning

Wash and cook spinach with seasoning but no extra water, until
tender (about 10 mins.).
White Sauce (thick)

1 oz. butter   1 oz. flour
¹/₄ pt. milk   Seasoning

Make sauce by heating butter then adding flour and cooking for
several minutes. Add the milk, bring to the boil and cook until
thick, stirring all the time. Season lightly. Strain spinach and
either sieve or chop. Blend with sauce; add sugar and nutmeg.
Keep until cold.

On each plate place a slice of smoked salmon, a
tablespoonful of cold scrambled egg, two/three tablespoonsful
of spinach mixture. Garnish with parsley. Serve with brown
bread and butter, if desired.

Serves 6   *Mrs. E. Inett, Berkswell*

JUBILEE SEAFOOD STARTER

Tomato Chartreuse

One 15 oz. can of tomatoes and liquid

$\frac{1}{4}$ bay leaf

Slice onion

2″ stick celery

Very small slice green pepper (optional)

Grated rind of $\frac{1}{2}$ orange

Squeeze of lemon juice

Salt, pepper and sugar

2 tspns. gelatine

—————

6 oz. raw smoked haddock fillet

2-3oz. peeled prawns

$\frac{1}{4}$ pt. mayonnaise made with 1 yolk, salt, pepper, mustard, $\frac{1}{4}$ pt. olive oil and lemon juice to taste

1 tbspn. tomato ketchup

$\frac{1}{2}$ tspn. chilli sauce (Amey) (beware, it's hot and gets hotter!)

3-4 tbspns. whipped cream (4 fl. oz. of cream)

$\frac{1}{2}$ tspn. wine vinegar

1 tbspn. chopped chives or a slice of onion put through a garlic press

1 tspn. chopped fresh basil or $\frac{1}{4}$ tspn. dried

1 tbspn. chopped parsley

Salt and pepper

Lemon juice

Soak gelatine in 2 tbspns. cold water in a small bowl and then stand in a saucepan of hot water to melt. Liquidise and sieve ingredients for Tomato Chartreuse, add gelatine, check seasoning and pour tomato jelly into 4 individual containers to come about half way up. Put aside to set. To make mayonnaise, beat egg yolk with salt, pepper and mustard in a bowl for 1 minute until thick and sticky. Gradually drop by drop beat in oil and finish with squeeze of lemon to taste.

Skin raw smoked haddock and cut into cubes, combine with prawns and squeeze over some lemon juice. Combine mayonnaise with tomato ketchup, chilli sauce, vinegar, chives or onion, parsley, basil and whipped cream. Mix with fish and preferably leave to mature for two hours. Spoon on top of Tomato Chartreuse, sprinkle with parsley and serve with brown bread and butter rolls.

Serves 4

Nicola Cox, Farthinghoe, Fine Wine and Food Ltd.

MEDITERRANEAN SQUID

2 lbs. squid
Butter
2 tbspns. oil
3 tbspns. chopped parsley

3 cloves garlic
1 tbspn. garlic powder (not garlic salt)
Seasoning

Prepare squid by pulling head from body and discarding sac and backbone. Slice body into rings. Separate head from tentacles — discard head.

Melt butter and oil, add garlic and garlic powder — saute squid, slowly with lid on for $\frac{1}{2}$ hour. Add salt and black pepper and half the parsley — turn up the heat and fry without the lid until the squid is browned and the sediment in the pan is crunchy. Add the remaining parsley and serve.

N.B. Do not wash the squid before cooking or most of the flavour will disappear down the drain.

Serves 2 — 4   *Mrs. J. Grant, Long Marston*

(s) # AVOCADO PEAR FILLING

1 tbspn. mayonnaise
2 tbspns. whipped cream
1 tspn. wine vinegar

1 tspn. sherry
Seasoning

Mix together and add prawns or crabmeat and serve at once in halved avocado pears.

Mrs. M. Sykes, Kenilworth

(E)(S)   ## LEFTOVER'S GASPACHO

Every hostess has found herself after a party with quantities of limp green salad which, because it has French dressing on it, seems only fit to be thrown away. However, if you put it in the blender, French dressing and all, add tomato juice and either tinned or fresh (peeled) tomatoes — the quantities will obviously depend on how much salad you have left over — with a small onion and a little crushed garlic, and blend it well you will have a delicious gaspacho. Serve it chilled with a little sour cream stirred in and a few croutons and every one will think you have spent hours preparing it!

Mrs. J. M. Macnair, Ullenhall

BROAD BEAN STARTER

1 lb. shelled young broad beans

4 rashers streaky bacon

3 hard boiled eggs

2 oz. can anchovy fillets

2 tbspns. snipped chives

¼ pt. French dressing (made with lemon instead of vinegar)

Cook beans in salted water until just tender. Drain and refresh. Cut bacon into small pieces and fry until crisp. Shell and chop eggs. Drain oil from anchovy fillets and divide each fillet into half lengthways.

Arrange the beans in a shallow serving dish and cover with the bacon pieces.

Mix chopped eggs and chives together and place on the bean mixture. Make a criss-cross pattern on top with the anchovy fillets. Chill. Before serving pour over the dressing. Serve with brown bread and butter.

Serves 6 — 8 *Ann Curtis*

Ⓢ ☆

PRAWN AND MELON MAYONNAISE

½ lb. peeled prawns

4 oz. green grapes, halved and pipped

½ honeydew melon, skinned and cut in squares

¼ pt. whipped cream

½ pt. mayonnaise (Hellman's)

2 tspns. curry paste

1 oz. tomato puree

Juice of 1 lemon

½ level tspn. of sugar

Salt, cayenne pepper.

Mix curry paste, tomato puree, lemon juice and sugar — leave to stand for an hour or so. Add this curry mixture to the cream and mayonnaise mixed together. Fold in the prawns and fruit, and serve with chopped parsley or chives sprinkled on top.

Serves 8   *Mrs. John Owen, Shipston-on-Stour*

Ⓢ

MELON AND GRAPEFRUIT COCKTAIL

1 medium sized melon in balls or small pieces

2 tins unsweetened grapefruit segments

French dressing

2-3 bunches watercress

Drain melon and grapefruit segments and mix with roughly chopped watercress. Combine with a good French dressing. Chill and Serve.

Delicious for a summer starter.

Serves 6   *Mrs. P. Scroggs, Warwick*

COURGETTES A LA TURQUE

1 large onion, chopped
2 tbspns. olive oil
1 ½ lbs. courgettes
4 eggs

10 oz. grated Gruyere or
   Cheddar and Parmesan
Salt and pepper
¼ pt. plain yoghurt
Pinch dried mint

Wash courgettes, trim and remove skin from the very large ones. Cut into ½ " slices and steam or poach until nearly tender. Drain and place in oven-proof dish. Sweat onion in butter and sprinkle over courgettes. Beat eggs, add grated cheese, salt and pepper to taste, pour over courgettes and bake in moderate oven (375°) for 20 mins. until top is lightly brown.

Serve with slightly salted yoghurt flavoured with dried mint.

Serves 4 — 6   *Nicola Cox, Farthinghoe,*
                                    Fine Wine and Food Ltd.

(S)
LEG OF PORK IN JELLY

5 lb. boned leg of pork   Chopped fresh herbs
1 glass of white wine   Spikes of garlic
Pepper and salt

Remove rind and cut into strips. Roll meat and tie into fat
sausage shape. Make four rows of incisions and press in herbs
and spikes of garlic, rolled in pepper and salt. Put into roasting
pan with bones and rind. Add white wine and water to half way
up meat. Cover pan and put in slow oven (330f). Cook for $3\frac{1}{4}$
hours. Remove meat, strain liquid into a bowl and leave to set.
Next day, remove fat from jelly. Carve meat into thin slices and
lay out in serving dish.

Surround and cover with jelly.

Serves 10   *Mrs. T. W. Beecham, Tidmington*

COLD PARSLEY HAM

2 lbs. cooked ham in piece   6-8 tbspns. fresh parsley
1 pt. well flavoured white   2 tbspns. gelatine
  stock   1-2 tbspns. tarragon
$\frac{1}{4}$ pt. dry white wine   vinegar
Freshly ground black pepper
  and nutmeg

Dice ham, simmer gently for 5 mins. in chicken or veal stock
and white wine with seasoning to taste.

Drain reserve stock and place ham in a wet glass bowl dusted
lightly with a little chopped parsley.

Soften gelatine in water and stir into hot stock. Add
remaining parsley and vinegar. Allow to cool until syrupy and
then pour over ham to cover.

Set for at least 12 hours.

Serves 6 — 8   *Mrs. P. Beney, Warwick*

(E)(S)   ## SICILLIAN LIVER

1 lb. approx. calves liver —   Black pepper
if possible — otherwise   1 tbspn. dry Vermouth or
lambs   wine
1 dspn. chopped rosemary   Butter

Wash the liver in warm salted water, skin and core then slice
finely. Melt butter or oil in pan, add chopped rosemary and
ground black pepper and fry liver gently, turn—it takes
seconds! Add about 1 tablespoon of Vermouth or wine to the
pan. Put liver on hot dish, pour sauce over, thicken if liked, and
serve at once with rice and salad.

Serves 4   *Mrs. J. Little, Shipston-on-Stour*

(S)   ## ROAST POUSSIN WITH
               ## FRESH HERB BUTTER

Four 12oz. poussins   4 oz. butter

Herb butter:

4 oz. butter   Salt and black pepper
Salt and pepper   2 tbspns. chopped mint,
2 large cloves garlic   marjoram, basil thyme,
                                fennel and tarragon.

Split cloves of garlic lengthwise and insert each half inside the
poussins with approx. $\frac{1}{2}$ oz. butter per bird. Liberally salt and
pepper the outer skin and spread the remaining butter over the
birds. Add 1 tbspn. water to the roaster - if possible a self-
basting roaster. Cover and place in the oven at 400°f for
approx. 30 mins., baste well and cook for a further 10 mins.
until the skin is golden brown. Remove the garlic and put the
poussin on a serving dish. Pour over the juices and place 1 oz.
herb butter on the breast bone whilst still hot, the butter melts,
leaving the herbs on the top of each bird. Serve with crisp green
salad, hot bread and eat with your fingers.

Serves 4   *Mrs. P. Beney, Warwick*

FASULYA

2 lb. of lean lamb uncooked	1 tbspn. tomato puree
1/2 lb. tomatoes, fresh or tinned	Salt and pepper
2 large onions	1/2 pt. of water approx.
2 cloves of garlic	1 lb. of French beans

Cut meat into small pieces discarding all fat and sinew. Wash and slice beans. Place lamb and beans in a casserole. Add the chopped tomatoes and onions with two cloves of crushed garlic. Mix the tomato puree, salt, pepper and water and add to the casserole. Cover and cook in the oven at 325°f (Mark 3) for 2 hours or until the meat is tender.

Serves 6　　　　　　　　*Mrs. A. Trye, Leamington Spa*

☆ SAO PAULO SHRIMPS

2 lbs. shrimps (defrosted and drained)	2 tspns. chilli powder
	2 tspns. sugar
2 medium onions, chopped very fine	1 tspn. oregano
	1 tspn. sweet basil
4 cloves garlic, crushed	2 tbspns. chopped parsley
3 tbspns. oil	Cooked rice
1 lb. tin of Italian tomatoes (drained and chopped)	Salt and pepper to taste
	2 oz. pine kernels (optional)
1 tbspn. lemon juice	

Cook the onions, garlic and oil in a saucepan until translucent.

Add tomatoes, lemon juice and seasoning and simmer for 20 mins.

Add the shrimps, parsley and simmer gently for a further 5 mins.

Serve on a bed of rice and pine kernels.

Serves 4 — 6　　　　　*Mrs. J. Jennings, Leamington Spa*

COLD DUCK IN JELLY

1 duck and giblets	2 bay leaves	2 oz. butter
2 oranges	2 stalks parsley	Lemon juice
3 carrots	1/4 oz. gelatine	Salt and pepper
3 onions	1/4 pt. white wine	1 egg white

Put giblets in pan with 1 onion, 1 carrot, bay leaf, parsley and salt. Cover with 1pt. cold water and cook for 1/2 hour. Strain, cool and remove fat.

Heat butter in large casserole or roaster with lid. Brown bird all over and remove. Chop and saute remaining vegetables and then replace duck. Pour over 1/2 pt. stock and wine. Cook in moderate oven (Reg. 4) until done. Approx. 70 mins. for 5 lb. duck.

Remove duck and leave to cool. Strain sauce and when cold remove fat. Clarify the liquid with the egg white. Season.

Peel orange and slice thinly pouring any juice into the sauce. Shake 1/4 oz. gelatine into sauce and stir well until dissolved.

Cool and strain. Place bird on dish with oranges around and coat with some of the jelly as it thickens. Set the rest and chop and arrange around the bird.

Serves 4

Mrs. P. Beney, Warwick

Ⓢ **COLD CHICKEN CRANWORTH**

Put 3 lb. chicken in roasting tin with a tumbler of white wine, butter, onions and cloves. When cooked, cool in the juice only removing when juice has jellied. Put jelly in liquidiser with half a pint of French dressing and half a pint of single cream - pour over chicken pieces and chill in 'fridge.

Serves 4

The Lady Cranworth, Suffolk

TURKISH CHICKEN

1 x 4 lb. roasting chicken, or chicken pieces

2 x 5 oz. cartons natural yoghurt

½ level tspn. ground ginger

½ level tspn. turmeric

½ level tspn. ground cumin seed

½ level tspn. chilli powder

1 level tspn. garam masala*

1 level tspn. salt

1 clove garlic

2 bay leaves

1 tspn. tomato puree

Grated rind of one lemon

Freshly ground black pepper

A little paprika

*Garam masala is a special blend of spices, which can also be used in curries; it is better to leave it out than to use a substitute.

Put the yoghurt into a large bowl and mix in the ginger, turmeric, cumin seed, chilli powder and garam masala. Peel the outer papery skin off the clove of garlic, slice it, and crush it with the salt, under the blade of a heavy knife, to a cream. Add this to the yoghurt mixture with the bay leaves, tomato puree, grated lemon rind and plenty of freshly ground black pepper.

Put the chicken pieces into this mixture and leave to become well saturated with the yoghurt and spices. Make quite sure that all the pieces are well coated, cover the bowl with a piece of polythene or foil and leave for at least 24 hours in a cool place.

Next day, remove the bay leaves. Put a wire rack into a roasting tin and place the chicken pieces on it. Spoon over the remaining yoghurt mixture and sprinkle a little paprika on top. Bake in oven at Gas Mark 4, or 350° for about 1½ hours until the chicken is tender and a crisp golden brown.

Serve with green salad and rice.

Serves 4 — 6   *University of Warwick, Women's Group*

⒮ VEAL CHOPS AND ROSEMARY

8 veal chops	1 wine glass of white wine
2 good sprigs of Rosemary	Salt and pepper
3 oz. butter	½ pt. of double cream

Trim the chops and roll in well seasoned flour. Heat the butter in a frying-pan and saute the veal for about 5 mins. on each side. Remove to a casserole dish. Add the wine to the pan and blend with the juices, season, add the rosemary and pour over the veal. Place in a moderate oven 300°f for about ¾ -1 hour, when meat should be tender. Remove rosemary and stir in the cream. Return to the oven for 5 mins. for the cream to heat through — but do not let it boil — and serve immediately.

Serves 8 *Mrs. J. Winstanley, Barford*

☆ POULET VALLEE D'AUGE

(Chicken cooked in Calvados cream — Normandy Fashion)

1 chicken	1 onion
2 oz. butter	½ bay leaf
8 oz. mushrooms	Thyme
3 tbspns. Calvados	Cup of double cream

Cut a fat chicken in pieces. Season. Fry pieces in butter for about 15 mins. or when about two-thirds cooked. Then add 8 oz. finely sliced mushrooms, one chopped onion, half a bay leaf, sprig of thyme. Cover pan and leave to cook in own juices, turning now and again until done. Add 3 tablespoons of good Calvados. Set alight and baste. Dish chicken up on warm dish and keep warm. Add a cup of fresh cream to juices in cooking pan, stir for a few minutes over heat with wooden spoon. Pour over chicken and serve piping hot.

Serves 4 *Mrs. D. White, Stratford-on-Avon*

Ⓢ   ## CHICKEN TONNATA

1 chicken	Lemon juice
1 tin anchovies	$^1/_3$ pt. olive oil
1 egg	4 oz. tuna fish
Pepper	Cold stock (if necessary)
Mustard	

Cook chicken, cool, remove meat from carcass and cut into bite-sized pieces. (If liked, insert six slices of anchovy under the chicken skin before cooking to add extra flavour).

Place the tuna fish, the rest of the tin of anchovies, the egg, seasoning and lemon juice in liquidiser, blend until smooth and then pour in the oil very slowly with the motor turned to its fastest setting. Blend until it resembles mayonnaise and add a very little cold stock if it is too thick.

Pour over the chicken and decorate with very thin slices of lemon and watercress bundles.

This is very good for summer buffet parties and much more economical than the classic veal tonnata.

Serves 4   *Mrs. J. M. Macnair, Ullenhall*

Ⓔ Ⓢ   ## QUICK TANGY
CHICKEN DRUMSTICKS

Chicken drumsticks	Seasoning
Soy sauce	Butter
Rosemary	

Place drumsticks in large frying pan containing melted butter, sprinkle them with soy sauce and rosemary and season according to taste. Fry gently, turning frequently until tender.

Serve with new potatoes and green salad.

Mrs. J. Hobbs, Kenilworth

(s) (☆)   ## CHICKEN BREASTS DIVINE

6 sliced chicken breasts	2 tbspns. dry Sherry
12oz. tin asparagus tips	2 tbspns. butter
1 tbspn. butter	2 egg yolks
2 tbspns. flour	Salt and black pepper
Milk	

Heat asparagus tips in butter, and place in oven-proof dish. Put chicken breasts on top and sprinkle with sherry. Make a roux with butter and flour, asparagus juice and milk if necessary. Beat in egg yolks, pour over chicken and bake at 350°f for 40 mins. or until chicken is tender, in covered dish. Serve with fried potato balls and salad.

Serves 6   *From a New Zealand girl*

(s)   ## MARIA'S FISH DISH

4 fillets of white fish	One 14 oz. tin tomatoes or
1 medium onion chopped	fresh tomatoes
1 clove garlic	2 level tspns. sugar
1 large green pepper (seeded)	1 tspn. oregano or marjoram
chopped	Salt, pepper to taste

Topping:

1 oz. grated cheese	2 slices bread, rubbed into crumbs

Wash and dry the fish. Put in a buttered shallow oven-proof dish. Fry the chopped onion and green pepper in a little oil for 5 mins. Place in a blender goblet with the remaining ingredients, blend until smooth. Pour over the fish and sprinkle cheese and bread crumb mixture on top. Bake in the oven at 375°f (Mark 5) for 45 mins.

Serves 4   *Mrs. R. Jennings, Leamington Spa*

COLD FISH MOUSSE

Made in blender

3 tbspns. lemon juice

2 tbspns. cold water

¾ oz. Davis's gelatine (1½ pkts.)

5 fl. oz. boiling fish stock

2 sticks celery roughly chopped

1 small onion roughly chopped

½ carrot roughly chopped

¼ med. cucumber peeled

1 tspn. chopped parsley

1 tspn. tomato puree

1 tbspn. anchovy essence

Blend with vegetables unless salmon is used

1 tspn. dill, if possible

¼ pt. mayonnaise

½ pt. double cream

1 lb. fish. Fresh Haddock, Cod - or Salmon if you have it left or are feeling extravagant, poached with skin and bones removed

Seasoning and 2 tbspns. Dry Sherry

Put in blender, lemon juice, cold water and gelatine and allow to sponge for 5 mins. Add boiling fish stock and blend well until gelatine is dissolved. Blend in vegetables herbs and seasoning. Pound fish well, mix all well together with slightly beaten cream and mayonnaise. Season well and stir in sherry. Set in fish mould and leave at least three hours to set.

Mrs. John Owen, Shipston-on-Stour

(E)(S)   ## MACKEREL SURPRISE

6 medium sized mackerel   1 pt. of gooseberry puree

Clean the mackerel and stuff with gooseberry puree. Wrap in buttered foil and bake in moderate oven (350°f) according to size of mackerel.

Serves 6   *Dame Margaret Shepherd, Herefordshire*

STUFFED FILLETS OF PLAICE WITH MORNAY SAUCE

4 fillets of Plaice (skinned)   4 oz. breadcrumbs
1 hard-boiled egg (chopped)   1 egg
2 tspns. chopped parsley   Salt and pepper
4 oz. chopped prawns

Sauce:

$\frac{1}{2}$ pt. bechamel sauce   4 oz. grated Cheddar cheese
$\frac{1}{2}$ tspn. made mustard   Salt and pepper

Mix together the hard-boiled egg, parsley, prawns and breadcrumbs. Add seasoning and mix in well beaten egg. Put this mixture onto the fillets of plaice and roll up. Place in well buttered oven-proof dish and cover with milk and the juice of 1 lemon. Cook in moderate oven for 15 mins. Remove, pour off the milk, and keep warm.

Using $\frac{1}{2}$ pint bechamel sauce made with the milk from the fish, add $\frac{1}{2}$ tspn. made English mustard and 4oz. of grated Cheddar cheese. Place fillets on oven proof dish and cover with the sauce. Sprinkle a small amount of cheese over each fillet and brown under the grill.

Alan Poole, The Three Shires Inn,
Serves 2   *Little Langdale, Cumbria*

✩ GALWAY HALIBUT

2 whole thick halibut steaks   1 small carton double cream
2 tbspns. oil and butter   Lemon slices for garnish
1 onion chopped   Salt and black pepper
4 tbspns. Irish whisky   2 tbspns. chopped parsley
Juice of 1 lemon

Melt the oil and butter in a frying pan and saute the onion.
Season the fish and fry about 5 mins. on each side. Pour in the
lemon juice and bring to the boil. Then add the whisky and
flambe. Simmer fish gently turning over once and basting well.
Remove fish and keep warm. Add cream to the sauce and stir
gently. Pour over the fish and garnish with parsley and lemon
slices.

Serves 4   *Mrs. R. Curtis, Alvechurch*

BLACKCURRANT CHARLOTTE RUSSE

1 lb. blackcurrants
1 ½ lb. apples
3 tbspns. water
2 oz. sugar
Juice ½ lemon
3 oz. sugar
½ oz. powdered gelatine
Few drops green colouring

1pt. milk
2 tbspns. custard powder
2 oz. sugar
4 tbspns. water
½ pt. whipping cream
24 savoy fingers
Little milk

Cook currants with sugar, no water. Remove few for decorating. Cook peeled sliced apples with water and lemon juice until pulp. Colour if wished. Blend little milk with custard, bring the rest of the milk to boil, pour over custard, return to pan to thicken with sugar and dissolved gelatine, cool, fold in cream. Stir half custard into apple puree and half into currants. Cool Dip fingers in milk and arrange round sides. Put cooled puree in layers in mould. Leave to set, turn out. Decorate with cream and blackcurrants, to vary, use other fruit.

Serves 8 — 10   *Mrs. A. Trye, Leamington Spa*

Ⓢ # BLACKCURRANT DREAMS

15 oz. freshly cooked or tinned
   blackcurrants
5 oz. carton hazelnut yoghurt

1 large egg white
2 tbspns. double cream
1 oz. chopped hazelnuts

Drain the blackcurrants, put the fruit in a blender with 8 tbspns. of juice and puree till smooth. Add cream and yoghurt and blend again. Whisk egg white until stiff. Fold in blackcurrant puree. Serve topped with whipped cream and a sprinkle of nuts.

Serves 4
                              Nicola Cox, Farthinghoe,
                              Fine Wine & Food Ltd.

(E)(S)(F)   **SUMMER PUDDING**

5-6 rounds stale white bread-unsliced	1½ lbs. mixed soft fruit - gooseberries, redcurrants, raspberries, blackcurrants, etc.
4-6 oz. gran. sugar	

Remove crusts from bread and cut 1-2 slices to fill the bottom of pudding basin. Arrange slices to line the sides, cutting if necessary, and keep 2 for the top. Put sugar and fruit in shallow pan and cook for 10-15 mins. Cool slightly and sweeten if necessary. Half fill the basin with fruit, place one piece of remaining bread and then spoon in enough mixture to fill the basin. Cover with the last piece of bread and fill basin with the remaining juice.

Place a saucer or plate on top with a 2lb. weight and leave over night.

This freezes very well.

Serves 6 — 8   *Mrs. P. Beney, Warwick*

⟨☆⟩ **BRANDIED OR VODKA PEACHES**

12 large peaches	1½ cups of water for syrup: boil for 10 mins.
1½ cups of sugar for syrup: boil for 10 mins.	Brandy or Vodka

Skin peaches in boiling water, halve and stone them. Place halves in wide-necked jar (2lb.). Pour syrup over fruit and leave for 12 hours. Pour a half or three quarters of the liquid off and top up the jar with brandy or vodka. Cover jars carefully.

Store at least 2 months in a cool dark place.

This sounds very extravagant but cheap brandy (Spanish perhaps) can be used and it's delicious as a winter party pudding.

Serves 8 — 10   *Mrs. J. Butterworth, Coventry*

[F] [☆]

CRUMBLY CHEESECAKE
with
BLACKCURRANT SAUCE

8 oz. semi-sweet biscuits
2 oz. butter
12 oz. curd cheese
4 oz. castor sugar
$\frac{1}{2}$ oz. packet of gelatine
Nutmeg - half tspn.

Juice of lemon
7 oz. double cream
3 egg whites
$\frac{1}{4}$ lb. blackcurrants a little
  water for the sauce

Butter the inside of an 8" flan ring. Melt the butter and add to already crushed biscuits and nutmeg. Put half the mixture at the bottom of the flan ring and place in freezer. Dissolve the gelatine in a little water; cream the curd cheese and sugar, add gelatine to the lemon juice and pour into the curd mixture, whipping at the same time. Whip the egg whites, fold in the cream, add the whites and pour the whole mixture into the flan. Sprinkle the rest of the biscuit crumbs over the top and chill. Cook the blackcurrants with a little water and sugar, sieve and serve as a sauce.

Serves 8 — 10 *Mrs. J. Winstanley, Barford*

[S] [F] ## GOOSEBERRY ICE CREAM

1 lb. fresh gooseberries   6 oz. sugar $\frac{1}{2}$ pt. double cream

Make a puree by cooking the gooseberries together with the sugar and sieve. Leave to cool. Whip cream lightly until it has thickened and fold into puree. Turn into basin or ice tray and freeze for approximately two hours until mixture has reached a mushy state. Remove from freezer, beat well, pour into waxed or plastic containers. Return to freezer for at least 3 hours before serving.

Mrs. P. Wartnaby, Leek Wootton

(E)(F) ## GOOSEBERRY SOUFFLE

½ lb. gooseberries   1½ tspns. gelatine
2 eggs   2½ fl. oz. whipping cream
2-3 scented geranium   4 oz. sugar, or to taste
  leaves or head of elder flower

Place gooseberries in a bowl with 3 oz. sugar, 2 tbspns. water and the scented geranium leaves; place the bowl, covered, over a saucepan of boiling water and cook until tender; strain off the syrup (there should be 2½ fl. oz.) into a small saucepan. Sprinkle gelatine over 2 tbspns. of cold water in a small bowl, soak for several minutes then place bowl in hot water until gelatine has dissolved; cool. Place egg yolks in Magimix or liquidiser and switch on, heat syrup to boiling then gradually pour into yolks. Whisk until pale and fluffy, add gelatine and set aside to cool.

Puree gooseberries with geranium leaves in liquidiser, sieve and cool.

Combine cooled yolk mixture with gooseberry puree and chill until cold and beginning to thicken; then add whipped cream and finally fold in egg whites whipped to a peak with 1 oz. of sugar beaten in as for meringues. Pour into 1pt. souffle dish and serve cold with little biscuits.

Serves 4   *Nicola Cox, Farthinghoe,*
                                Fine Wine and Food Ltd.

(S) ## FRESH STRAWBERRIES

Hull strawberries and place on a bed of finely crushed ice. Leave two small saucers beside the strawberry bowl and fill one with icing sugar, the other with thick cream mixed into a coffee liqueur.

Spear strawberries and dip each one first into sugar and then into the cream

Simple and delicious.

Mrs. P. Beney, Warwick

☆ SPECIAL STRAWBERRY TORTE

8 oz. Sugar	6 oz. plain chocolate
4 egg whites	1 pt. double cream
Pinch of salt	2 cups fresh strawberries
1/4 tspn. cream of tartar	2 oz. castor sugar

Beat egg whites, salt and cream of tartar until stiff then add sugar and beat again. Line flat baking tins with grease proof paper. Trace three 8″ circles with a pencil. Spread meringues on circles about 1/4 ″ thick. Bake 20-25 mins. at 250°f. Remove from oven. Peel off paper. Cool on cake rack.

Melt over hot water: 6 oz. plain chocolate, 2 tbspns. water.
Whip 1 pt. double cream and add 2 oz. sugar.
Slice 2 cups of fresh strawberries. Place on serving plate.
1 meringue layer
Spread thin coating of chocolate mixture
Spread 1/2 ″ layer of cream
Put 1/3 of the strawberries on top.
Repeat the layers and top with the third meringue. Spread remaining cream round the sides and decorate with fresh strawberries. Put in refrigerator for at least 2 hours.

Serves 8 — 10   *Mrs. B. Weber, Solihull*

⒮ MELON WITH RASPBERRIES

Charantais or Ogen Melon	2 tbspns. sugar

1/2 lb. raspberries, hulled

Cut through centre of melon and scoop out seeds. Cut again into quarters and then remove peel. Slice like an apple into serving dish. Sprinkle with 2 tbspns. sugar and chill well to draw the juices. Fold in 1/2 lb. fresh raspberries and serve cold for a dessert.

Serves 6   *Mrs. P. Varley, Leamington Spa*

Ⓢ   ## GOOSEBERRY FLAN

Rich shortcrust pastry   3 oz. castor sugar
1 ½ lb. Gooseberries   1oz. flour
4 fl. oz. double cream   ½ tspn. ground cinnamon

Line 8″ flan ring with pastry.
    Cover with gooseberries.
    Stir into the cream the sugar, flour and add cinnamon.
    Pour over gooseberries and bake at 470°f for 10 mins. and
then at 375°f for further 20 mins.

Serves 6   *The Lady Cranworth, Suffolk*

Ⓢ ☆   ## GRANITA DI CAFFE

2 ½ heaped tbspns. ground coffee
1 pt. boiling water

Pour water onto coffee. Allow to stand. Strain and sweeten
while still warm.
    It should now taste like Italian expresso coffee.
    At this stage a sliver of lemon may be added, but do
remember to take it out before you start the freezing.
Alternatively a dash of brandy, which is very effective. Put the
liquid into the freezer and after an hour or so, when it reaches a
mushy state, stir it to remove the icicles. Remember to get it out
of the freezer half an hour before serving, otherwise you will be
excavating for it!
    Serve with whipped cream.
    Delicious after a rich course: it acts as a sorbet.

Dr. Judith Rawson, Department of Italian,
University of Warwick

BLACKCURRANT TRIFLE

Put 4 wedges of sponge cake at bottom of bowl, dampen with 2 tbspns. sherry and cover with thick layer of fresh blackcurrants sieved to puree ½ pt. (not over-sweetened).

Add layer of creme patissiere — when cooled:—

1 oz. flour	Vanilla essence
1½ oz. sugar	1 pt. milk
1 whole egg and 1 yolk	

Mix flour, sugar, egg and egg yolk, vanilla essence smoothly and add to boiling milk. Bring to boil again, remove from heat and whisk briskly. Cover creme layer with whipped cream and serve chilled.

Serves 6   *Mrs. C. Sykes, Kenilworth*

E S F   **MERINGUE CREAM**

Broken meringues - up to 18	¼ pt. double cream
Grated rind of 1 orange	Sugar to taste

Whisk cream until stiff, flavour with orange rind and sugar. Fold in broken meringues. Pour into oiled cake tin or mould, cover with foil and freeze. 10 mins. before serving, dip mould into hot water and turn out, and serve with fresh summer fruit.

A marvellous way of using up the meringues that go wrong - which they frequently do!

Serves 6 — 8   *Mrs. C. G. Moira, Stareton*

HAZELNUT ROLL

3 oz. ground hazelnuts
2 oz. cornflour
1 tspn. baking powder
3 eggs
4 oz. castor sugar

$^1/_2$ pt. double cream
$^1/_8$ pt. single cream or milk
2 bananas or raspberries or strawberries in season

$^1/_2$ oz. grated plain chocolate, 12 hazelnuts - for decoration

Prepare oven Mark 5 or 375-400°f. Prepare swiss roll tin, line with paper. Mix ground nuts, cornflour and baking powder. Whisk eggs and sugar till "rope-like". Fold in hazelnut mixture and spread into prepared tin. Bake for 10 to 15 mins. until firm to touch. Turn out onto dredged paper or cooling tray. When cool, fill with sliced banana or fruit, cream and roll up. Decorate and serve chilled.

Serves 6   *Mrs. T. F. Horn, Warwick*

⌊s⌋

QUICK SICILLIAN
SPAGHETTI SAUCE

¹/₄ pt. olive oil
1 can anchovy fillets, finely
  chopped
One 15 oz. can of tomatoes
8-12 tbspns. finely
  chopped parsley

1-2 cloves of garlic,
  crushed
2 oz. chopped walnuts
4 oz. chopped raw fresh
  mushrooms
Salt and pepper

Combine oil and anchovies in pan. Heat gently stirring and mashing the anchovies against the side of the pan until blended. Drain tomatoes and chop coarsely. Add to pan with chopped parsley and other ingredients. Heat through and season. DO NOT COOK the sauce only heat it through, and serve with cooked spaghetti.

Mrs. R. Dunn, Bonsall

(E)(S)   RUNNER BEAN SALAD

¹/₂ lb. runner beans	Salad oil
One 13 oz. can flageolet beans	Sea salt
1 tbspn. grated onion	Black pepper
1 clove garlic	1 chopped hard-boiled egg
Lemon juice	Chopped herbs

Prepare and slice beans in the usual way. Do not use old, tough beans!

Cook beans in boiling salted water and cook until just tender. Drain and refresh. Gently toss beans with oil, salt and pepper. Add flageolet beans, grated onion, crushed garlic and lemon juice. Add more salt and pepper if necessary. Serve with chopped hard-boiled egg and herbs scattered over the top.

Serves 8 — 10   *Mrs. R. Curtis, Alvechurch*

(E)(S)   POLISH BEETROOT

2 lbs. cooked beetroot	¹/₈ pt. milk
Small onion (finely chopped)	1-2 tbspns. vinegar
2 tspns. horseradish cream	Seasoning
¹/₂ oz. butter	Parsley
¹/₂ oz. flour	

Grate beetroot.

Melt fat and fry onion, stir in flour, add milk and bring to boil.

Add beetroot and vinegar and horseradish. Heat and season. Dish and decorate with chopped parsley.

Serves 8 — 10   *Mrs. C. Sykes, Kenilworth*

[E] [S] COURGETTES ANGLAIS

½ lb. pork sausages ¾ pt. cheese sauce
1 lb. courgettes 4 eggs

Wipe and slice the courgettes and plunge into lightly salted boiling water. Cook for 5 mins. and then blanch in cold water. Meanwhile make up ¾ pint of cheese sauce. Divide the sliced courgettes into four small fire-proof dishes then place sausage pieces (cut in half) on top. Break an egg into each dish. Add salt and pepper to taste. Pour over cheese sauce adding a little grated cheese over the top. Cook in medium oven for 20 mins. until brown.

Note: Spinach can also be used in this recipe as a substitute for the courgettes, a good supper dish.

Serves 4 *Mrs. M. Orton, Barford*

[E] [S] PICNIC SLICE

8 oz. milk chocolate or 1 beaten egg
 cooking chocolate 4 oz. dessicated coconut
2 oz. butter or margarine 2 oz. sultanas
4 oz. castor sugar 2 oz. glace cherries

Melt chocolate over hot water in basin and pour onto greased swiss roll tin approx. 11" by 7", and allow to set. Cream fat and sugar, add beaten egg, then coconut, sultanas and cherries. Mix well and spread over chocolate. Bake in slow oven at 310°f. for about 45 mins. until golden brown.

Serves about 8 *Mrs. P. Howell, Kenilworth*

---

⑤ SPICY COURGETTES AND BEANS

Equal quantities of very
    small courgettes and very
    young French beans
Olive oil

1 small chopped onion
Garlic (optional)
1 tbspn. soy sauce
Sherry

In a heavy pan fry the onion and garlic slowly in the oil. Add
the sliced courgettes and beans and continue cooking over
increased heat stirring all the time to coat them well in oil. Add
the soy sauce and continue to stir - fry for another minute.
Lower heat, add a dash of sherry and continue cooking, stirring
frequently until the vegetables are just tender but still crisp.

Mrs. J. M. Macnair, Ullenhall

SALAD DRESSING

2 tbspns. castor sugar
1 tspn. mustard
$\frac{1}{2}$ tspn. salt
Shake of pepper
1 egg

Mix all together

Add 2-3 tbspns. vinegar
Add 2 tbspns. milk

Mix. Allow to stand half an hour before serving to let sugar
dissolve.

Mrs. J. Benn, Tredington

SPINACH TART

2 lb. fresh spinach
1 ½ oz. butter
1-1 ½ oz. flour
½ pt. creamy milk
2 cloves garlic
1 oz. Gruyere cheese, grated

Butter
Salt
Plenty of freshly ground
  pepper
½ lb. shortcrust pastry

Make pastry well in advance and chill.

Cook spinach in a covered saucepan with a sprinkling of salt but no extra water, drain well for at least 15 mins. Make a smooth bechamel sauce and add the crushed cloves of garlic, salt, pepper and cheese. Line a flan case with pastry and bake the tart shell for 15-20 mins. blind in a moderately hot oven Reg. 6/400.

Mix the chopped spinach into the sauce, which can be quite thick as the spinach holds a lot of water. Pour into the flan case. Bake at Reg. 6/400 for 20 mins. until lightly browned. Very good cold.

**For lunch for 4 or
dinner for 2 — 3**   *Mrs. P. Scroggs, Warwick*

E S CARROTS WITH LEMON SAUCE

1 lb. carrots

Sauce:

1 tbspn. cornflour
4 teaspoonfulls sugar
¼ tspn. salt
2 tbspns. butter

4 oz. water
3 tbspns. lemon juice
1 tspn. grated lemon rind

Mix sugar, cornflour and salt in saucepan. Blend with half the water until smooth. Add remaining water. Cook, stirring constantly, until mixture boils. Remove from heat, add remaining ingredients.

Scrape carrots and cut into shape desired - matchsticks, rounds, etc. Boil until just tender with a little salt. Drain and mix with sauce. Let stand until time to serve, then re-heat quickly over hot water.

Mrs. R. Weber, Solihull

Autumn

"... to bend with apples the moss'd cottage tree,
And fill all fruit with ripeness to the core,"

Keats.

AUTUMN RECIPES

Starters

Main Courses

Puddings

Miscellaneous

SALADE des MOULES

4 lb. (1 ½ kilograms) mussels
1 shallot
1 glass white wine

Pilaff

4 oz. (125 gm) rice	Butter
1 onion	Parsley
4 oz. (125 gm) white mushrooms	Mussel liquor, made up to ½ pt. (3 decl.) with stock
½ head of celery	1 tbspn. oil
4 tbspns. cream	Seasoning
Lemon juice	Parsley

Scrape mussels and wash well in cold water. Chop shallot finely and fry in butter in a large pan, add wine, seasoning and parsley stalks and bring to boil. Add mussels, cover pan and cook briskly for 4-5 mins., until mussels are open. Drain off liquor and reserve.

Prepare pilaff

Chop onion and fry in oil until soft, add rice and fry for 2-3 mins. Add ½ pt. mussel liquor (made up with stock if necessary), cover and cook gently without stirring for 20-25 mins. Cool.

Slice mushrooms and sprinkle with lemon juice. Chop celery into ½ " pieces.

Remove shells and beards from mussels. Combine with vegetables. Stir into rice when cold together with cream and seasoning. Decorate with parsley.

Serves 8   *Mrs. J. Cozens Horley*

STUFFED AUBERGINES

2 Aubergines
4 tbspns. oil (or more)
1 oz. butter or margarine
1 clove garlic
1 tspn. mixed herbs
Seasoning

4 medium sliced onions
4 large ripe tomatoes -
  peeled, pipped and coarsley
  chopped
Parmesan cheese
Brown bread crumbs

Cut aubergines in half lengthwise and criss-cross flesh. Sprinkle with salt and leave for 30 mins. Drain and dry, fry face down in oil for about 7 mins. do not brown, turning once or twice, and adding more oil, if necessary.

Lift out and scrape all the meat carefully from the skins; chop coarsely.

Melt the butter, add onions and sweat — do NOT brown, add tomatoes, garlic, aubergine meat, herbs and seasoning, simmer for 5 mins. Fill skins with the mixture, dust well with cheese and bread crumbs, brown under the grill or in the oven.

(Will freeze, may also be eaten cold, sliced, as a vegetable)

Serves 4

SARDINE PATE

Tin of sardines in oil
6 oz. Philadelphia cream
  cheese

Lemon juice
Black pepper

Drain oil off sardines and remove backbones. Mash all ingredients together very well. Put in refrigerator. Serve cold with hot buttered toast.

Do not blend as it becomes too liquid.

Serves 6   *The Hon. Mrs. Smith Ryland*

MUSHROOM PARMESAN

Mushrooms picked from the fields if possible, otherwise from the local market stall.

For 1 lb. mushrooms (ie. 8 persons)

4 tbspns. grated Parmesan cheese

8 tbspns. freshly made breadcrumbs

2 tbspns. chopped Parsley

4 tbspns. chopped shallots (previously softened in butter)

Wash and peel the mushrooms and put in a shallow fire-proof baking dish.

Sprinkle with salt and pepper. Add the shallots, the parsley and cheese.

Finally cover thickly with the breadcrumbs, dot across the top small pieces of butter or margarine.

Bake for 15-20 mins. in a moderate oven.

Garnish with parsley sprigs and serve.

Serves 8   *Mrs. J. Butterworth, Coventry*

SMOKED MACKEREL PATE

1 lb. smoked mackerel fillets

½ lb. cream cheese

Tabasco

Salt and pepper (black freshly ground)

Juice of 2 lemons

Marinate the fish in lemon juice for at least three hours.

Skin the fillets and put in liquidiser goblet with the lemon marinate and all the other ingredients. Blend until smooth, check seasoning and spoon into souffle dish. Chill — sprinkle top with paprika and serve with fingers of toast.

Serves 8   *Mrs. J. M. Macnair, Ullenhall*

Ⓢ Ⓕ
SALMON MOUSSE

8 oz. tin red salmon   Lemon juice
$\frac{1}{4}$ pt. double cream   Salt and pepper
$\frac{1}{2}$ oz. gelatine   1 egg white

Pound salmon and add lemon juice. Add gelatine to liquid from salmon and place over pan of hot water. Stir until dissolved. Add to salmon. Lightly whip cream and add to salmon. Beat egg white and add to mixture. Turn into oiled ring and chill until set. Ideal for freezing.

(Slightly extravagant but quick and delicious)

Serves 4 — 6   *Mrs. P. Wartnaby, Leek Wootton*

GREEN PEPPER AND HAM RAMEKINS

3 eggs $\frac{1}{4}$ lb. cooked ham
$\frac{1}{4}$ pt. double cream   Black pepper and a little salt
$\frac{1}{2}$ pt. milk   Cheese and breadcrumbs
1 green pepper finely   mixed for top
  chopped and blanched

Beat eggs with milk, cream and black pepper and salt. Add pepper and ham and put in 8 ramekin dishes which have been buttered. Sprinkle with mixture cheese and coarse white breadcrumbs. Cook gently in oven until just set (300°f.)

If necessary put under hot grill to brown for about 1 min. (Do not allow to boil in oven or it will separate).

Serves 8   *Mrs. J. Owen, Shipston-on-Stour*

WHITE ONION SOUP

1 lb. onions	1 oz. plain flour
½ oz. butter	2 beef stock cubes
1 tbspn. oil	Salt and pepper

Peel and finely slice the onions. Heat butter and oil in a large saucepan and add the onions. Fry slowly for 8-10 mins. until golden brown, then stir in flour and cook for 1-2 mins. Stir in 2 pts. of cold water and stock cubes, bring to the boil and simmer for 10 mins.

Serves 6 — 8 *Mrs. J. Dunnett, Chadwick End*

SOUTHERN TOMATO SCRAMBLE

1 green pepper chopped small	1 tspn. sugar
1 medium onion chopped small	1 oz. butter
	1 tbspn. olive oil
1 lb. tomatoes skinned and quartered, or one 14oz. tin of drained tomatoes	1 clove garlic
	1 small tin sweet corn
	1 tbspn. double cream

Cook onion gently in butter and oil until transparent. Add pepper and cook for further few minutes. Add tomatoes, sweet corn, garlic, salt, pepper and sugar, and simmer. Just before serving add 1 tablespoonful double cream. Good hot or cold as a starter or just as a lunch dish with crusty French bread.

Serves 4 *Mrs. F. Wigley, Warmington*

☆ SHOULDER OF LAMB WITH HAM AND SPINACH FILLING — SERVED WITH STUFFED TOMATOES

3-3 ½ lbs. shoulder of
   lamb
8 oz. fresh spinach
2 oz. onion
3 oz. butter
Small handful of parsley
   (chopped)

Pinch of tarragon (chopped)
6 oz. cooked ham, diced
1 oz. breadcrumbs
2 eggs, beaten
Salt and pepper
Bone the shoulder

Wash spinach. Place in saucepan over medium heat for 5 mins. to sweat without adding more liquid. Drain and press spinach well. Chop onion, saute in 2oz. butter. Chop parsley. Add spinach, parsley, tarragon, ham, breadcrumbs and stir in eggs. Cook for 2 mins. Season.

Stuff shoulder with this mixture. Season joint. Dot with remaining 1 oz. of butter and roast for 1½ hours at 350°f Gas Mark 4.

Stuffed Tomatoes:

1 lb. frozen peas
2 oz. single cream
6-8 tomatoes

1 oz. butter, to glaze
2 lb. young carrots to garnish

Wipe tomatoes — halve and remove seeds. Season and bake at top of oven for 10 mins. Cook and cool peas. Drain and press through sieve or liquidiser.

Season puree and beat in cream. Fill tomato halves with mixture. Re-heat in oven for 5 mins.

Cook and cool carrots. Toss in butter and garnish the joint.

Serves 6 — 8   *Mrs. J. Butterworth, Coventry*

(E) (F)   ## POOR MAN'S MOUSSAKA

2 lbs. minced lamb belly or   1 lb. courgettes
    middle neck, stripped of fat   1 pt. stock
2 large Spanish onions   ½ pt. cheese sauce
2 cloves garlic   McDougalls Bolognaise
Olive oil for frying   Sauce Mix
1 lb. potatoes   Salt and pepper

Make the meat sauce the day before — or morning before.
Chop the onions and fry in oil until golden. Squeeze garlic
through a press and fry with onion for one minute.

    Add 2 heaped tbspns. bolognaise sauce mix and stir in. Then
add minced meat and stock and stir up. Cook for ½ hour. Leave
to get cold.

    Parboil potatoes and drain. Cut the courgettes into three inch
chunks and cook in salted water until nearly tender. Drain.

    Line a buttered fireproof dish with slices of potato. Add
alternate layers of meat mixture and courgettes and finish off
with potato. Make a white cheese sauce and pour over the
whole lot and grate a little cheese on top.

    Now it can be put in the deep freeze or cooked for ¾ hour in
a moderately hot oven.

Serves 6   *The Lady May Sibford Gower*

(S)   ## PHEASANT OR
CHICKEN CASSEROLE

1 jointed chicken or pheasant   Rosemary
Continental liver sausage   Thick creamy white sauce
    garlic

Put jointed chicken and slices of liver sausage in dish, pour over
white sauce. Sprinkle with Rosemary and cook in low oven
350° for about an hour.

Serves 4   *Mrs. J. Butterworth, Coventry*

☆ ROAST WILD DUCK

2 wild ducks	4 strips of bacon
2 cloves	$1/_3$ pt. apple juice
2 small onions	$1/_3$ pt. orange juice
2 one-inch pieces of salt pork	$1/_2$ cup of "rough" port
$1 1/_2$ tspn. salt	2 tbspns. grated orange rind
$1/_2$ tspn. ground black pepper	$1/_2$ tspn. thyme
	3 tbspns. melted butter

Hang the ducks for three days. Wash and dry them. Stick a clove into each onion and place one onion and one piece of salt pork in each duck. Season ducks with salt and pepper. Cover the breasts with the bacon. Place in a roasting tin.

Mix together the apple juice, orange juice, port and thyme, and pour over ducks.

Roast in oven of 350°f for one hour or until tender — test by pressing back of spoon onto breast. Baste frequently during roasting period.

Just before serving: Remove bacon. Brush birds with mixture of butter and Worcester sauce. Leave for 5 mins. in oven to "crisp" skin.

Transfer ducks to hot serving dish.

Thicken gravy with arrowroot.

Serves 4 — 6   *Mrs. J. Butterworth, Coventry*

LIVER WITH DUBONNET AND ORANGE

1 lb lamb's liver	4 fl. oz. red Dubonnet
1 tbspn. olive oil	2 tbspns. finely chopped
1½ oz. butter	parsley
2 shallots or small onions	Coarsely grated rind of 1
1 clove garlic	large orange
Seasoned flour	1 tspn. finely grated lemon
1 tbspn. orange juice	rind

Cut liver into ½ inch thick slices. Heat the oil and butter in a large frying pan. Cook the very finely chopped onions and the crushed garlic, covered, over a low heat, until the onions are soft and beginning to colour. Coat liver slices with seasoned flour and put them in the pan in one layer. Continue to cook over very moderate heat. As soon as the blood rises, turn the liver and cook it for a rather shorter time at an even lower heat. Remove the slices to a warm plate and keep them hot.

Add the orange juice and Dubonnet to the onions and juices left in the pan, scraping the bottom with a wooden spoon or spatula. Bring to the boil and cook rapidly for a few minutes until the sauce has reduced by half. Strain it and return it to the pan. Lower the heat and add the parsley, orange rind and lemon rind (keeping some of the orange rind and parsley for a garnish) and stir the sauce until it reaches boiling point. Pour it over the liver and serve at once.

Serves 4 — 6   *Mrs. P. Scroggs, Warwick*

ⓢ AUSTRALIAN CHICKEN

Chicken portions (1 per
person)
Butter
Honey

Stem ginger
Almonds, blanched and
chopped

Place chicken portions into buttered pyrex dish. Spread each portion with honey and then cover with the stem ginger juice and a few ginger pieces.

Cover with tin foil and bake in oven at 350°f for 1 hour 15 mins. Remove tin foil and sprinkle with chopped almonds and brown in oven at 400°f.

The Hon Teresa Pearson, Gloucestershire

⬡ MARINADED VENISON

2½-3 lbs. venison

Marinade:

2 cups red wine
2 cups water
1 clove garlic, crushed
1 tbspn. chopped onion
1 tbspn. chopped carrot

1 tbspn. chopped celery
A few sliced mushrooms
8 peppercorns
Bay leaf

Soak the hung venison from 36-48 hours, turning it from time to time in the marinade.

The longer it marinates, the better. Roast in oven with marinade below venison. Baste frequently and cook for 1½-2 hours at 375°f. Strain liquid through sieve, thicken with a little flour and add 1 gill sour cream or yoghurt. Either serve separately or slice roast meat, arranged on dish with sauce poured over. Decorate with watercress or chopped parsley.

Serves 6   *Mrs. P. Beney, Warwick*

☆ SPICED PORK

A hand of pork 3-4 lbs.	1 clove garlic
10-12 juniper berries	2 bay leaves
1 tbspn. sea salt	Couple of fennel stalks
1 tspn. peppercorns	2 slices of lemon
$\frac{1}{2}$ tspn. cummin seeds	$\frac{1}{2}$ pt. white wine or cider

Skin and bone the joint (or get the butcher to do it for you!) and cut off the trotter. Crush together salt, pepper, cummin, garlic and juniper berries and rub well into the meat. Tie the joint into a good roll, lay it in a casserole with the skin underneath and put the bones and trotter around it; tuck in the bay leaves, lemon slices and fennel stalks and leave for 2-12 hours in a cool place.

Add wine and enough water to cover the meat. Cover with greaseproof paper and a lid and cook in a very low oven 270° for 2-5 hours until soft when prodded with a skewer. Remove joint and cool. Simmer stock and bones for another hour before passing through a sieve and you will have a bowl of beautiful, strong stock to use as a base for soups and sauces. Serve the thinly sliced meat cold with saute potatoes and salad. If you prefer to serve the sliced meat in jelly, de-fat the cold jelly stock and boil $\frac{3}{4}$ pt. down to $\frac{1}{2}$ pt., flavour with lemon juice, sherry or Madeira, strain through muslin and, when cold, pour oven the sliced meat.

Serves 10 — 12

Nicola Cox, Farthinghoe,
Fine Wine and Food Ltd.

Ⓔ Ⓢ   **LAMB BOULANGER**

1 shoulder lamb — 4-5 lbs.	½ pt. stock
Seasoning, herbs, garlic	1 tspn. (tomato) puree.
2-3 lbs. potatoes, peeled and sliced	1-2 tbspns. oil
	Parsley - chopped
2-3 large onions, peeled and sliced	2 aubergines - sliced
	4 large tomatoes, peeled and sliced

Bone shoulder and season well.

Sprinkle with thyme and garlic. Roll up and tie.

Brown meat in oil. Remove. Slice onions and brown. Layer onion and potatoes in large oven-proof dish. Place meat on top, arranging the remaining vegetables around. Mix stock and puree and pour over meat. Season well.

Cook covered, Mark 4, 350°f for 2-2½ hours.

Serve sprinkled with parsley.

Serves 8   *Mrs. V. Graham, Offchurch*

☆   **AUSTRIAN VEAL**

½ lb. veal (shoulder or leg)	¼ pt. water
4 oz. mushrooms	1 tspn. paprika
4 oz. tomatoes peeled and sliced	¼ lb. cooked rice
	4 oz. grated cheese
2 oz. lard	1 oz. butter

Cut veal into thin slices. Brown in lard, stir in paprika, add a little water and simmer for 5 mins. Slice mushrooms and simmer slowly in butter for 10 mins. Arrange layers of meat, rice, mushrooms and tomatoes ending with rice in casserole. Sprinkle with grated cheese. Bake in moderate oven for 15 mins.

Finish under grill.

Serves 4   *Mrs. B. Inett, Berkswell*

☆   **SEAFOOD PIE**

Cheese Pastry:

8 oz. S. R. flour   3 oz. finely grated cheese
4 oz. margarine and lard
    mixed

Filling:

6 oz. cooked and boned   Salt and pepper
    smoked haddock   1 tbspn. cream
3 oz. scampi   1 glass white wine
2 oz. prawns $\frac{1}{2}$ pt. bechamel sauce,
2 oz. cooked and sliced   peppercorns and bay leaf
    mushrooms $\frac{1}{2}$ oz. flour and butter
1 egg yolk

Make sauce, add wine, cream and other ingredients. Season.
Make pastry, bind to a stiff paste with egg and water. Line 7″
flan ring with half of the pastry, add filling and cover with
remaining pastry. Decorate, brush with egg to glaze and bake at
400°f.

Serves 4 — 6   *Mrs. R. Bradley, Machynlleth, Wales*

Ⓕ ☆   **PHEASANT WITH CELERY
                    AND WALNUTS**

2 oven ready pheasants   4 oz. butter
1 lb. button onions   3 tbspns. flour
6 rashers back bacon   1 pt. stock
1 good head celery   3 wineglasses red wine
2 oz. shelled roughly chopped   Thyme, bay leaves parsley
    walnuts   and seasoning
1 tbspn. oil

Peel the onions, dice the bacon and chop the celery in $\frac{3}{4}$″ slices.
Fry the bacon until crisp, and set aside. Add the oil to the pan

and brown the pheasants all over. Place in large casserole dish. Saute the onions with the rest of the fat in the pan for a few minutes and, together with the bacon, add to the casserole. Pour into casserole the stock, wine, herbs and seasoning, cover and cook in a moderate oven for about an hour. Meanwhile melt 2 oz. of butter in a frying pan and cook the celery and walnuts until crisp. Sprinkle with salt and leave. Joint the cooked pheasants and arrange on an attractive dish. Strain the stock, but scatter the onions and bacon over the pheasant. Make a roux with the remaining 2 oz. of butter and the flour, gradually blend in the stock, simmer for a few minutes before pouring over the pheasant. Garnish the dish with the celery and walnuts.

Serves 6 — 8   *Mrs. J. Butterworth, Coventry*

☆   **PORK PAPRIKA**

2-3 pork fillets (about 2 lbs)	Sherry
1½ oz. butter	½ pt. consomme or stock
2 shallots or 1 small onion	6 oz. button mushrooms
1 dspn. paprika	1 level dspn. cornflour
1 dspn. flour	½ pt. thick cream
	1 tspn. tomato puree

Cut fillets into thick medallions, saute in hot butter until lightly browned, and place in casserole. Add finely chopped onion and paprika to the butter in pan and cook gently for one or two minutes, then stir in flour, tomato puree, sherry and consomme. Stir until boiling, check seasoning and pour over the pork. Cover and put in oven 300°f until it comes to the boil, reduce heat to 225° and simmer for about 1 hour until meat is tender. Cool and leave over night to obtain best flavour. To complete, re-heat gently thicken with cornflour if necessary, add mushrooms, and just before serving add cream and serve very hot, with noodles and salad.

Serves 6 — 8   *Mrs. P. Breyfogle, Stareton, Warwickshire*

MRS. MAC'S PHEASANT

1 pheasant
1 lb. eating apples, peeled
   cored and sliced
Butter
Seasoning

A little brandy or white wine
   (optional)
Stock
1 onion — finely chopped
$\frac{1}{4}$ pt. double cream

Soften onion with butter in a heavy casserole. Add the apple slices and place the pheasant on top, dot with butter and moisten with a little stock and the alcohol if used. Cover casserole tightly and cook in a moderate oven (300°f) for about an hour, basting occasionally.

Joint pheasant and place on serving dish and keep hot. Pour the apple and onion mixture into a liquidiser, blend, add the cream, blend until smooth, adjust seasoning and pour a little sauce over the pheasant. Serve the rest separately.

This recipe is very suitable for any game, particularly birds that may not be in their first youth! Cook for longer at a lower temperature if you are using old birds.

Serves 3 — 4   *Mrs. J. M. Macnair, Ullenhall*

⌊E⌋ ## JELLIED RABBIT MOULD

1 rabbit — from which flesh
   has been removed and cut
   into small pieces
2 oz. bacon
Seasoning

$\frac{1}{2}$ pt. water or stock
Grated rind of $\frac{1}{2}$ lemon
Grated nutmeg
1 tspn. chopped parsley
$\frac{1}{2}$ oz. gelatine

Mix rabbit meat, bacon, seasoning and pack into oven-proof mould.

Dissolve gelatine in stock and pour over meat to cover completely.

Cover with foil and cook in oven at 350°f for 1-1$\frac{1}{4}$ hours. If stock has diminished, refill to cover and leave to set. Serve with a salad.

Serves 6 — 8   *Mrs. M. Sykes, Kenilworth*

CHICKEN GOUGERE

Choux pastry made with:-
7$\frac{1}{2}$ oz. plain flour, 6 oz.
    butter, $\frac{3}{4}$ pt. water 4 eggs.

2 oz. diced cheese (Cheddar)
One 3$\frac{1}{2}$ lb. chicken poached in
    well flavoured stock
$\frac{1}{4}$ lb. button mushrooms

1 large Spanish onion,
    chopped
1 clove garlic, crushed
4 tomatoes
2 oz. butter
2 oz. flour
$\frac{3}{4}$ pt. stock (from poaching
    the chicken)
Grated Parmesan

Make up the choux pastry in usual way and stir in diced Cheddar. Grease a good sized gratin dish and use pastry to form a thick border around the edge.

Soften onion and garlic in the butter, add flour, cook 1-2 minutes then add stock and continue stirring over heat until sauce thickens. Remove from heat and add sliced mushrooms and quartered, peeled and de-seeded tomatoes. Adjust seasoning. Chop the chicken into large dice and fold gently into sauce. Pour mixture into centre of choux pastry ring and sprinkle with Parmesan. Bake in a hot oven 425°f (Mark 7) for 20 mins., to puff pastry then reduce heat to 325° (Mark 4) for another half an hour until dish is golden brown. Serve with a green salad.

Serves 6   *Mrs. H. Lambert, Welford upon Avon*

FLAKY VEAL ROLL

E

1 onion
2 cloves of garlic
1 ¼ lb. pie veal
1 tbspn. oil
1 level tspn. chopped fresh
  tarragon, or ¼ level tspn.
  dried tarragon

Salt and ground black
  pepper
1 tspn. Worcester sauce
1 large egg
¾ lb. flaky pastry

Peel the onion and garlic mince together with the veal.

Heat the oil in a frying pan and add the minced ingredients.

Turn the mixture with a spatula over a moderate heat for about 2 mins. to seal the meat.

Add the herbs. Season well with salt, black pepper and Worcester sauce.

Beat the egg, add to the meat mixture, allow to cool.

Heat oven (450°f. Gas Mark 8, centre shelf.)

Roll out the pastry to a narrow oblong, about 16″ by 6″.

Place the mixture in the centre of the pastry, shaping it to a long sausage.

Brush all the edges of the pastry with water or beaten egg.

Roll up the pastry so that the join comes underneath the roll, seal the ends.

Put the roll on to a damp baking sheet and bend the roll round to form a "horseshoe".

Make slits at intervals in the pastry with a sharp knife.

Bake for 10 mins.

Reduce oven temperature to 400°f. Gas Mark 6 and cook the roll for a further 35 mins.

Serves 6 — 8

(E)

COD CHOWDER

1 ½ lb. cod	1 pt. milk
3 rashers bacon	1 oz. flour
1 onion	1 ½ oz. butter
3 stalks celery	Chopped parsley
2 lb. potatoes	

Fish stock

Cod trimmings	2 stalks celery
1 onion	1 pt. water
Bay leaf	

Put ingredients for stock in saucepan, bring to boil and simmer 30 mins and strain. Meanwhile cut bacon into small pieces and fry until crisp. Chop vegetables.

Add extra fat to pan if necessary and saute vegetables.

Pour on the fish stock and season and simmer until vegetables are nearly cooked.

Cut fish into squares, dredge with the flour and add to pan with the milk and butter and simmer for a further 10 mins. Season and serve sprinkled with parsley.

Serves 4 — 6 *Mrs. M. Sykes, Kenilworth*

⒠ BLACKBERRY MERINGUE TORTE

Base:

5 oz. plain flour   2 oz. castor sugar
3 oz. butter   2 egg yolks

Meringue filling:

1½ lb. blackberries   ½ pt. double cream
2-4 oz. castor sugar   A few extra berries for
  (depending on tartness of   decoration
  fruit)

First make up the pastry base. Sift flour into bowl and make a well in the centre, chop butter into walnut sized pieces and put in the well with the sugar and yolks, work it all together with the fingertips very lightly until it forms a smooth dough. Refrigerate for ½ an hour. Roll out to form a large circle, about 10″ in diameter, place on a baking sheet, pinch around edges to form a pattern like shortbread and prick with a fork. Bake for 25-30 mins. 375° Reg. 5 until golden. Cool.

Whisk egg whites until really stiff and then add 2 tbspns. castor sugar and continue whisking until smooth and glossy, then fold in remaining sugar. Pipe large rosettes of meringue around pastry base forming a wall and bake in a very cool oven to dry out the meringue — about 1½ hours. This can be done in advance and stored in an air-tight tin.

When ready to serve, whip cream and fold in fruit and sugar. Pile mixture into centre of ring and decorate with the extra fruit.

Serves 10   *Mrs. H. Lambert, Welford upon Avon*

PEACH CARAMELS

5 peaches   2 tbspns. milk
$\frac{1}{2}$ pt. whipped cream   1 tbspn. butter
1 cupful brown sugar

Peel peaches, cut in half and remove stones. Fill peach centres
with whipped cream, join halves and secure with cocktail stick.

Put sugar, butter and milk in pan, stir until boiling and
simmer for 7 mins. Beat until beginning to thicken, pour over
peaches.

When cold remove sticks. Top each with swirl of cream and
chopped nuts.

Serves 5   *Mrs. M. Sykes, Warwick*

ⓢ **BLACKBERRIES WITH BANANAS**

4 bananas   3 oz. castor sugar
Lemon juice   Whipped double cream
1 lb. blackberries

Slice bananas and squeeze lemon juice over these. Put in
shallow gratin dish.

Add blackberries.

Sprinkle with 2 oz. castor sugar.

Cover with cream and put in 'fridge.

At last minute sprinkle with remaining sugar and brown
under grill.

Serves 4 — 6   *Mrs. D. Peachey, Kenilworth*

APRICOTS WITH CREAM
AND BRANDY

1 oz. butter
2 oz. castor sugar
2 lb. (approx.) tin of
   apricots

2 tbspns brandy
¼ pt. double cream
Juice and grated rind of
   1 orange

Melt the butter in a large frying pan, and add the sugar. Stir
until the sugar has melted and the mixture is a golden caramel.
Add orange juice and rind and stir until mixed. Drain apricots
from juice and add to pan. Turn the apricots gently and allow to
become glazed with syrup. Add brandy and flame. Draw pan
off heat and pour in cream. Stir to blend sauce.

Serve hot with sponge fingers.

Serves 8   *Mrs. R. Curtis, Alvechurch*

Ⓔ   **BRAMBLE MOUSSE**

1 lb. blackberries
3 eggs
1 oz. castor sugar
3 oz. castor sugar
½ oz. gelatine

Juice of ½ lemon
2 tbspns. water
¼ pt. double cream (plus
   cream to decorate)

Stew blackberries with 1 oz. sugar. Sieve. Put eggs into bowl
over hot water with 3 oz. sugar and whisk until thick. Cool and
continue whisking.

Soften gelatine with water and lemon juice and stand in hot
water to dissolve.

Add gelatine to egg mixture. Fold in 6 oz. blackberry puree.
Fold in cream.

When set pour over extra puree, pipe on cream in lattice
pattern.

Serves 4   *Mrs. D. Peachey, Kenilworth*

☆ GATEAU NORMAND
(This is a delicious French pudding)

2 lbs. apples peeled and
   thickly sliced
4 egg yolks
1 egg
8 oz. cream
$\frac{1}{4}$ tspn. grated nutmeg
$\frac{1}{4}$ tspn. cinnamon

1 oz. sugar
1 oz. butter
$1\frac{1}{2}$ oz. flour
$\frac{1}{2}$ pt. milk
Pinch salt
1 glass Calvados

Beat egg and yolks together. Add flour, mix and beat well. Add milk gradually with sugar, cinnamon, nutmeg and salt. Add cream and Calvados.

Put apples in buttered oven-proof dish, pour mixture on top and cook for 45 mins. at 400°f.

This is better hot, but can be eaten cold.

Serves 6   *Mrs. A. Pritchett. Ullenhall*

ⓢ LEMON POSSET

$\frac{1}{2}$ pt. double cream
4 oz. castor sugar

Finely grated rind and juice
   of 1 large lemon
4 tbspns. good dry sherry

Measure cream, sugar, grated lemon rind, strained lemon juice and sherry into mixing bowl. Whisk all together until quite thick and then into individual glasses and decorate with chocolate sugar strands. If beaten for too long it will curdle.

Serves 4   *Mrs. P. Varley, Leamington Spa*

(E)
BLACKBERRY WITH
APPLE PANCAKES

Pancakes

8 oz. plain flour   Pinch of salt
3 eggs $\frac{1}{2}$ tspn. castor sugar
1 pt. milk   1 oz. melted butter

Filling

2 lbs. blackberries $\frac{1}{2}$ lb. or so apples   Sugar to taste

Make the pancake batter in the usual way, adding the melted butter last. Leave for 3-4 hours in a cold place. Cook the blackberries, apple and sugar with as little water as possible and set aside. Make the pancakes when required, fill with blackberries — serve with a squeeze of lemon juice and castor sugar on top of each pancake.

Serves 8 — 10   *Mrs. J. Winstanley, Barford*

(E)(S)
APPLE CRISP

1 lb. cooking apples   2 oz. castor sugar   1 tbspn. water

For the topping:

2 oz. butter or margarine   3 cupfuls cornflakes
1 rounded tbspn. golden
  syrup

Slice apples and arrange over base of pie dish. Sprinkle with sugar and add water. Put butter and syrup in pan over low heat. Stir until butter has melted. Take off heat and add cornflakes. Stir with fork until cornflakes are covered with syrup. Spoon over apples. Put into the centre of pre-heated oven (Gas 4) and bake for 20 to 30 mins. until fruit is tender and topping golden. Cool until topping is crisp and serve with cream or ice-cream.

Serves 4   *Mrs. P. Varley, Leamington Spa*

(F)

PINEAPPLE CHEESECAKE

1 lb. cottage cheese	$\frac{1}{4}$ pt. cream
8 oz. tin pineapple	3 oz. melted butter
Rind and juice of 1 lemon	8 oz. digestive biscuits
2 eggs	$\frac{1}{2}$ oz. gelatine
4 oz. sugar and 2 oz. castor sugar	

Sieve cottage cheese. Grate rind and squeeze juice of lemon and add to cheese.

Strain pineapple juice and add chopped pineapple to cheese. Place basin over pan of hot water. Add pineapple juice and gelatine, stir till dissolved.

Separate eggs. Mix yolks with 4 oz. of sugar till paste and then add to pineapple juice. Stir with wooden spoon till slightly thickened. Beat cream and add to cheese then beat white of eggs and add to cheese.

Base:
Crumble digestive biscuits with 3 oz. melted butter and 2 oz. sugar. Put base into a 9″ loose bottom cake tin (well oiled); press firmly into base. Add cheese mixture on top. Place in 'fridge to set. Ideal for freezing.

Serves 8   *Mrs. P. Wartnaby, Leek Wootton*

ⓢ ☆ **SUPER BRIE SAVOURY**

1 whole Brie (ripe but not
    too runny)
2 tins artichoke hearts (or
    bases)

Salt and black pepper
Hot French bread

Stand Brie on a large flan case or oven-proof platter suitable for serving. Cut a 6″ round from the centre and fill the space with the drained artichoke hearts. Sprinkle with salt and pepper. This can all be done earlier in the day. Ten minutes before serving place in a hot oven 425°f. Reg. 7. Serve immediately with chunks of French bread.

N.B. It is possible to obtain whole Bries 8″ in diameter for smaller parties and though it sounds very extravagant there is no need to have either a pudding or cheese course when serving it.

Serves 14   *Mrs. H. Lambert, Welford upon Avon*

Ⓔ **BLACKBERRY CURD**

2 lb. blackberries
2½ lbs. icing sugar
½ lb. butter

2 lemons
¾ lb. apples
6 eggs

Simmer together the apples (peeled and cored) and the blackberries until fruit is soft. Pour through sieve into double saucepan, add the juice of 2 lemons, butter and icing sugar. When it has all melted add eggs well beaten and continue cooking until mixture thickens. Bottle and seal as for lemon curd.

Good as filling for meringue layers.

Mrs. T. Abell, Tredington

(E) RICE AND MUSHROOM CASSEROLE

1 large onion, sliced (½ lb.)	1 tin condensed mushroom
2 oz. butter	soup, undiluted
1 tin beef consomme	1 lb. mushrooms, sliced
	1 cup long grain rice

Cook onion in butter until clear. Put into casserole and add rest of ingredients. Mix. Bake 1 hour at 325°-350°. Stir about every 20 mins. and add water if needed.

This can be made up early in the day and baked just before eating or baked early and warmed up.

Good with chicken, fish, etc. and tossed salad.

Mrs. B. Weber, Solihull

(E)(S) APPLE JELLY

2 lbs. cooking apples	½ pt. water
4 oz. or 4 rounded tbspns.	1 orange or lime or
caster sugar	greengage jelly

Peel core and slice apples. Measure sugar and water and stir over low heat to dissolve. Add the sliced apples, cover pan and simmer until soft. Draw pan off heat and add jelly in pieces. Stir until dissolved. Pass through sieve, stir and leave to set.

Mrs. R. Dunn, Bonsall, Derbyshire

BEEF BABOTIE

1 lb. minced beef
1 onion
Tomato puree
Curry power
Handful of dried fruit
1 glass red wine

Jam or marmalade
Pepper and Salt
1 yoghurt or sour cream
1 egg yolk
1 egg

Chop and saute onion in oil add wine — tomato puree (as for bolognese sauce) and a touch more of wine if too dry. Add 1 dessertspoon jam or marmalade, dried fruit — and only about a teaspoon of curry powder as it is just a very mild curry dish. Put all this mixture in a baking dish.

Mix yoghurt with eggs and pour over the top. This can also have grated cheese on the top.

Bake until the custard topping is set and browned.

Mrs. M. Carr, Rowington

(E) ## GREEN TOMATO CHUTNEY

3½ lbs. green tomatoes
2 tbspns. dry mustard
1 dspn. curry power
½ lb. apples
1¼ pts. of vinegar

½ lb. sultanas
1 tspn. cayenne pepper
1 lb. brown sugar
4 medium sized onions
1 tspn. allspice

Slice tomatoes and onions, sprinkle with salt, leave overnight and then strain. Place vinegar, sugar, mustard, and spices in a pan and boil. Put tomatoes, onion, apples and sultanas through the mincer and then add to the boiling vinegar. Boil until soft (½ -1 hour) and then bottle in the usual way.

Makes approx. 7lbs. *Mrs. P. Beney, Warwick*

(S)
CHOCOLATE SAUCE

8 oz. milk or plain chocolate   2 small tins evaporated milk
   block

Melt chocolate in bowl over hot water. When dissolved add evaporated milk. Serve hot or cold.

    This sauce can be used either for profiteroles or hot on ice-cream and is deliciously fudgey.

Mrs. J. Smith, Kenilworth

GRAN'S CHUTNEY

1 ½ lb. sour apples   Herbs
1 ½ lb. onions   ¾ pt. vinegar
1 ½ lb. figs and dates, mixed   Seasoning
2 lb. tomatoes   Spices

Put a bunch of mint, parsley and thyme, 2-3 bay leaves, 5-6 cloves, an inch of whole ginger, crushed, a dessertspoonful of pickling spice into a muslin bag and simmer in ¾ pt. of vinegar.

    Meanwhile peel and chop the other ingredients and add these to the vinegar remove the muslin bag and boil well. Add a little sugar if desired.

    Mix a dessertspoonful of salt, teaspoonful of pepper, ground ginger, ground spice, 1 oz. of dry mustard and a pinch of cayenne pepper and blend to a soft cream with a few spoonfuls of the boiling mixture. Add to the pan and stir in thoroughly for a few moments. Remove from the heat. Allow to cool and put in clean dry jars.

Mrs. D. Steel, Lancashire

Winter

"The Summer hath his joys, And winter his delights."

Thomas Campion.

WINTER RECIPES

Starters

Main Courses

Puddings

Miscellaneous

ⓢ KIPPERS IN CREAM AND CURRY

1 lb. kipper fillets	1 dspn. curry powder
1 bay leaf	1 small eating apple
Water	2 oz. flour
2 oz. butter	1 gill double cream

Poach the kipper fillets in $1\frac{1}{2}$ pts. water with the bay leaf.

Melt butter in a saucepan. Grate the apple straight into the butter and add curry powder. Sprinkle in the flour to make a roux and stir for 2-3 mins. until the flour is fully cooked. Slowly pour in 1 pt. of stock from the poached kippers and bring to boil stirring briskly. Simmer for 15 mins. before removing from heat. Blend in the cream. Flake in the kippers and ladle into 4 ramekins. Put a spoonful of cream on the top of each dish and flash under grill.

Eat immediately.

Serves 4   *Mrs. J. Terry, Wasperton*

ⓔⓢ BEST PARTY TOMATO BOULLION

1 large tin (32 oz.) tomato juice	3-4 cloves
4 tins consomme (undiluted)	3-4 peppercorns
1 onion, chopped	1 bay leaf
$\frac{1}{2}$ tspn. celery seeds	1 tspn. chopped parsley
	Salt to taste

Simmer 20 — 30 mins.
  Strain.
  Serve very hot.

Serves 8 — 10   *Mrs. R. Weber, Solihull*

CHESTNUT SOUP

A special effort for a winter dinner party

(F)

2 lbs. chestnuts

2 pts. stock — chicken is
  good

1 pt. milk

2 dspns. of flour

2 tbspns. cream

1 oz. butter

Sugar, salt and pepper to
  taste

Slice tops of chestnuts place in hot oven for 5-8 mins. Remove outer and inner skins. This is nail breaking work — though lots of helpers soon clear the task — puree of chestnuts (from France) can be bought in tins. The fresh chestnuts give a special flavour — probably nail flavour!

Put chestnuts, stock, salt and pepper into a casserole and simmer until chestnuts are tender (about 45 mins.). Cool and then liquidise. Return to casserole. Add the milk. Boil together, Fork together the flour and the butter. Add gradually to the casserole and stir until smooth.

Season — try a little brown sugar as well as salt and pepper.

Add the cream. Serve at once.

Serves 8 — 10   *Mrs. J. Butterworth, Coventry*

(E) (S)   **PEA AND HAM SOUP**

3 pts. ham stock   ¹/₂ lb. dried split peas, preferably green

Put peas and stock into pressure cooker, bring slowly up to 15 lb. pressure and cook for 45 mins. Add salt if necessary; if too salty peel two potatoes and boil in the soup for a quarter of an hour or so.

Serves 6 — 8   *Mrs. G. Holroyde, Warwick*

Ⓔ Ⓢ ROSY POTATO AND LEEK SOUP

1 lb. leeks	Salt and pepper to taste
1¼ oz. butter	1¼ pts. water
8 oz. tomatoes, roughly chopped	4 tbspns. cream
	Lemon juice to taste
2 tspns. sugar	2 tbspns. chopped parsley or chives
12 oz. potatoes, peeled and diced	

Wash and slice leeks thinly. Melt butter in a large saucepan, add leeks and cook over a low heat until soft but not coloured. Add tomatoes and sugar, cover and continue cooking until soft. Add potatoes and season well with pepper and salt. Add the water, cover and simmer gently for 30 mins. or until the potatoes are tender. Puree in blender or sieve. Stir in cream and sharpen to taste with lemon juice. Heat thoroughly but do not boil.

Sprinkle with parsley or chives.

Serves 8   *Miss Yvonne King, Redditch*

Ⓔ Ⓢ Ⓕ WATERCRESS VICHYSSOISE

5 potatoes	1 ham bone (optional)
2 large leeks	½ pt. cream
2½ bunches watercress	Salt and pepper
2 pts. chicken stock	

Cook sliced vegetables with ham bone in stock. Puree in a blender or through a sieve. Season and chill. Just before serving, stir in chilled cream.

This is a good way to use up old potatoes and leeks and freeze to use in the summer.

Serves 6   *Mrs. J. Butterworth, Coventry*

SMOKED HADDOCK PANACHE

1½ lbs. smoked haddock   1½ lbs. spinach
4 hard-boiled eggs   Butter
6 large tomatoes

Cheese sauce made with:-

1 oz. butter   ½ pt. milk
1 oz. flour   Salt and pepper
2 oz. grated cheese

Place the haddock in a large saucepan of water and bring to the boil and cook until tender and flesh will flake. Drain and cool fish. Peel and slice tomatoes. Cook spinach and drain, forcing out as much water as possible. Season well and add butter.

Put the spinach into a buttered dish, next the flaked fish, then the sliced eggs and finally the tomatoes. Season well.

Make the cheese sauce and pour over the top. Extra grated cheese may be sprinkled over and the pie then cooked in a slow oven 300-310°f. for half an hour.

Good as a supper dish.

Serves 6 — 8   *Mrs. R. Curtis, Alvechurch*

(E)(S)   **SMOKIE STARTER**

Skin, bone and flake 2 smokies into well buttered ramekin dishes. Drain a tin of tomatoes, and place one tomato per dish on top of the fish.

Barely cover with thick cream into which has been stirred a little malt whisky and seasoning. Sprinkle with grated Parmesan cheese and put in hot oven for 5 mins. Slide under the grill for a few moments until golden and sizzling.

Serves 4   *Mrs. J. M. Macnair, Ullenhall*

(F) **TURKEY LIVER PATE**

1 lb. turkey livers	2 tbspns. brandy
8 rashers streaky bacon	2 tbspns. port or sweet
¼ lb. mushrooms sliced	sherry
6 shallots — finely chopped	Mixed herbs
½ lb. butter	Salt and black pepper

Cut the rinds off the bacon and fry over a low heat. When enough fat has run out, add the shallots and mushrooms. Cook gently for about 5 mins. and then remove from pan. Add a little butter to the pan and gently fry the livers. Sprinkle the livers with mixed herbs whilst cooking, and when cooked put them through a fine mincer with the bacon, shallots and half the mushrooms. Chop the other half of the mushrooms to add to the pate. Whilst melting the butter, add the brandy and port to the minced mixture and beat with a wooden spoon. Pour in the butter and continue to beat. Then season well. Pour into individual dishes or a pate dish. Garnish with a little aspic or seal with melted butter if you wish and very finely chopped parsley.

Serve with hot brown toast and butter.

This pate improves after keeping in the refrigerator for 3-4 days for the flavour to develop.

Serves 12   *Mrs. J. Winstanley, Barford*

(s) (☆) ## PHEASANT CASSEROLE

2 pheasants	Bouquet garni
4 rashers streaky bacon	Seasoning
$\frac{1}{4}$ lb. mushrooms	2 tbspns. flour
16 approx. small onions	$\frac{1}{2}$ -$\frac{3}{4}$ bottle red wine (a
1 oz. butter and a little oil	good wine is better)
2 cloves of garlic	

Chop bacon, skin and prepare onions whole. Clean mushrooms. Melt oil and butter, cook onions and bacon until golden brown, add mushrooms. Cook for a further 2-3 mins. and put in casserole, adding herbs, chopped garlic salt and pepper. Roll pheasants in seasoned flour and fry until golden brown in remaining oil and butter. Place in the casserole, pour over wine and put in the middle of low oven at 300°f. for 3-3$\frac{1}{2}$ hours.

Serves 8 *Mrs. P. Drury-Lowe, London*

(s) ## BAKED HAM WITH ORANGE SAUCE

3-4lb. piece of ham	1$\frac{1}{2}$ tspns. mustard
Juice and rind of three	6 tbspns. clear honey
oranges	Brandy (optional)

Boil ham until nearly tender, for 20 mins. to the lb. Remove rind whilst hot. Make the glaze by creaming together the mustard, honey orange juice and rind.

Pour this over the ham and bake at 400°f. for 20-30 mins. basting at intervals. Remove meat and pour sauce into saucepan; rinse sediment from baking tin with a little water, add to the sauce, thicken with arrowroot and finally add brandy to taste.

Serves 6 —8 *Miss Anna Butterworth, Coventry*

Ⓔ Ⓢ   **FRESH HADDOCK
        IN MUSHROOM SAUCE**

1 lb. fresh haddock   1 oz. butter
2 limes or 1 lemon   Tin of mushroom soup
2 onions   Tin of button mushrooms

Cut and sprinkle haddock with lemon. Slice onions and put in
pan with butter, add soup, then haddock and put mushrooms on
the top. Cook at simmering point for $3/4$ hour.

Serves 3 — 4   *The Hon. Mrs. Smith Ryland, Sherbourne*

POCHOUSE

2 lbs. cod   3 shallots
$1/2$ pt. white wine   4 streaky bacon rashers
2 cups cream   Bouquet garni
2 oz. butter   2 tbspns. brandy
3 egg yolks   2 oz. flour
2 cloves garlic   Salt and pepper

Place the fish in a lidded frying pan. Add the wine, garlic and
bouquet garni, and simmer until cooked. Lightly fry the bacon
and onion which have been finely chopped. Add the Cognac
and flame.

   Put the fish onto a serving dish and keep warm. Remove the
bouquet garni from the liquor in which the fish was cooked.
Make the sauce by melting the butter and adding the flour.
Gradually add the cooking liquor and when blended stir in egg
yolks off the heat. Finally add cream and season well. Sprinkle
the onion and bacon mixture over the fish and coat with the
sauce.

N.B. Do not allow sauce to boil after egg yolks and cream have
been added.

Serves 6   *Mrs. R. Curtis, Alvechurch*

APRICOT ALMOND SALAD

1 onion	Apricot fruit from recipe above
2 oz. butter	
12 oz. Patna rice	1 small can red peppers
2 pts. bacon stock	3 oz. browned almonds
4 tbspns. French dressing	

Finely chop onion. Cook gently in melted butter until just beginning to brown.

Add washed rice and cook, stirring frequently, until brown. Add stock, mix well, season to taste. Simmer until all stock is absorbed and rice is cooked. When cold add cut up apricots, sliced peppers, coarsely chopped almonds and French dressing.

Mrs. J. Snook, Kenilworth

(E) (S)   **TURKEY AU GRATIN**

turkey left-overs (also suitable for fish or chicken)

2 level tbspns. butter	2 tbspns whipped cream
2 level tbspns. flour	1 beaten egg
1/4 pt. milk	Fresh breadcrumbs
1/4 pt. double cream	Butter to brown

Melt two level tbspns. butter in saucepan, add 2 level tbspns. flour and cook until roux is just golden. Add 1/4 pt. of milk and cook until sauce is reduced to almost half of the original quantity. Stir in 1/4 pt. double cream. Add 1/2 pt. of this sauce to flaked turkey leftovers. Season to taste with salt and pepper and pour into heat-proof dish. Combine remaining sauce with 1 beaten egg, fold in two tbspns. whipped cream and spread over turkey mixture. Sprinkle with fresh breadcrumbs, dot with butter and brown in hot oven (450°f.) or under the grill.

Serves 4   *Mrs. P. Wartnaby, Leek Wootton*

117

Ⓢ **MARCH PORK CASSEROLE**

1 small green pepper	One 8 oz. can tomatoes
2 oz. bacon dripping	Pinch mixed herbs
1 onion peeled and chopped	1 tspn. curry powder
1 leek washed and chopped	$\frac{1}{2}$ tspn. salt
2 oz. mushrooms	$\frac{1}{2}$ tspn. pepper
1 $\frac{1}{2}$ lb. hand or shoulder pork diced	1 oz. flour

Remove stalks and seeds from pepper and chop it. Melt the fat and fry onion, leek, pepper and mushrooms for 3 mins., transfer to casserole

Add curry, salt and pepper to flour and toss pork in this mixture. Fry the coated pork for 5 mins, stirring well, then put into casserole with vegetables, tomatoes, and herbs. Cover tightly and cook for 1 $\frac{3}{4}$ hours in a moderate oven.

Serves 4 *Miss Anna Butterworth*

Ⓔ Ⓢ **OXTAIL**

1 oxtail, cut into pieces and trimmed of excess fat	3 carrots, peeled and sliced (optional)
1 large onion peeled and sliced	

Put oxtail pieces in large oven-proof casserole. Spread the onions and carrots on top and cover with cold water. Season lightly with salt, black pepper and bay leaf. Cook in moderate oven for 2-3 hours, until meat is tender. Allow to get completely cold. Skim off fat and re-heat, thickening the gravy with one tablespoon of cornflour blended with a little cold water and stirred in.

Serve with jacket potatoes and spring cabbage.

Serves 4 *Mrs. P. Beney, Warwick*

(S)

COTES DE PORC SAVOY

4 pork chops	1 dspn. flour
1 lemon	½ pt. sherry,
2 oz. sultanas	Cider or Madeira
1 large apple	Stock if necessary
2 oz. butter	Seasoning

Brown chops in butter and place in oven-proof dish. Add the flour to the fat in the pan and brown gently. Add the sherry or Madeira and grated rind of the lemon, sultanas and the apple, peeled cored and sliced. Season well and add to the chops. Cook in a moderate oven (Reg. 4 or 350°) for 45 mins. to 1 hour.

Serves 4   *Mrs. A. M. Tulip, Kenilworth*

(E)(S)

LEEK AND LAMB

8 rotten old chump chops	Pinch of mixed herbs
6 large leeks	White pepper
Leek soup	Oil for frying
Stock	2 oz. butter
Garlic	

Wash and cut leeks into ¾ " pieces green ends as well. Melt 2oz. butter in a large saucepan and toss the leek in this until it is all covered with butter. Add 3 heaped tablespoons of Knorr leek soup (or any other you like) and mix well. Add 1 pt. of good stock, white pepper, pinch of herbs and simmer for ½ hour.

Meanwhile, salt and pepper chops and fry in garlic flavoured oil to seal them thoroughly. Drain. Put ½ leek mixture into a large casserole and place the chops on top and then cover with leeks and the rest of mixture. Cook in a moderate oven for 1 hour.

This is not a dainty dish but good winter filling food. It can be made just as well with pork spare rib chops.

It is cheap.

Serve 4 — well.   *The Lady May, Sibford Gower*

☆

VEAL OLIVES IN
SHERRY SAUCE

For the veal olives:

2-3lbs. lean veal

½ lb. mushrooms

2 large onions

1 tbspn. lemon juice

4 tbspns. fresh white bread
  crumbs

3 oz. butter

Salt and pepper

For the sauce:

2 oz. butter

2 oz. flour

¾ pt. chicken stock

¾ pt. milk

Sherry to taste

Salt and pepper

Prepare 16 well hammered pieces of veal. Peel and slice onions, and slice the mushrooms. Heat half of the butter in a frying pan and saute the onions and mushrooms, sprinkling with lemon juice and salt, until soft but not brown.

Blend in liquidiser or Mouli until smooth. Mix this with the breadcrumbs, and spread over each of the pieces of veal. Roll each one up and secure with a cocktail stick. Heat the rest of the butter in the same frying pan and cook the veal rolls for 10 mins., turning all the time to seal the meat.

Remove into casserole dish. Make a roux with the butter and flour, adding stock and milk, season, simmer for a few minutes, then remove and add the sherry. Pour over the veal and place in a moderate oven to simmer for ¾ hour-1 hour.

Serves 6 — 8   *Mrs. J. Winstanley, Barford*

Ⓔ Ⓢ　　　　**MEXICAN BEEF PIE**

8 oz. shortcrust pastry
2 tbspns. oil
1 onion (chopped)
1 lb. minced raw beef
Salt

Black pepper ($\frac{1}{4}$ tspn.)
1 dspn. of chilli powder
1 can tomatoes
Stuffed olives

Pre-heat oven to 400° Mark 6.

Line pie plate (9″) reserving pastry for decoration. Heat oil and saute onions. Add beef and cook, stirring frequently. Add seasoning and tomatoes and cook for 15 mins. Leave to cool a little. Turn mixture into pastry case. Roll out remaining pastry and cut into thin strips. Arrange over meat in lattice pattern. Bake for 35-40 mins. or until pastry is browned.

Serves 6　　　　　　*University of Warwick, Womens' Group.*

Ⓢ Ⓕ　　　　**FAMILY STROGANOFF**

2$\frac{1}{2}$ lbs. lean braising steak
1$\frac{1}{2}$ lbs. chopped onion
1 large clove garlic —
　creamed
$\frac{1}{2}$ pt. stock
Oil and butter

1 wine glass of sherry
$\frac{1}{4}$ tspn. paprika
$\frac{1}{2}$ tspn. salt
6 oz. sliced button mushrooms
$\frac{1}{2}$ tbspn. Worcester sauce
$\frac{1}{4}$ pt. soured cream

Cut beef into 2″ by $\frac{1}{2}$″ strips approx. and saute. Remove into casserole. Sweat onions and add to meat. Add everything but the mushrooms and cream, and cook for about 2 hours at about 300°f. Then add the mushrooms which have been cooked in butter and cook a little longer together. Thicken with a little arrowroot and serve with the soured cream stirred in.

Serves 6　　　　　　*Mrs. J. Allday, St. Owen's Cross*

(E) (S)   **HASH**

Always make extra gravy on Sundays with the joint and keep in 'fridge till needed

½ -1pt. gravy from roast   1 onion sliced
Bone, skin, and gristle
from leftover joint

Put all ingredients in 2 pt. saucepan or casserole dish and boil vigorously for at least 1 hour. Strain liquid.

Meat left over from joint   4 small onions quartered
1½ -2 lb. potatoes peeled
    and sliced

Replace liquid in pan and slice potatoes into it also add quartered onions and cook over moderate heat until potatoes are cooked, about ½ hour. Season.

Add chopped meat left over from joint about 10 mins. before end of cooking.

The liquid should be absorbed so the end result should be fairly thick.

Spoon into clean warm casserole and serve with pickles.

Variation — Add 1 tin of frankfurters instead of meat.

Serves 4   *Mrs. P. Beney, Warwick*

(F) CASSEROLE OF BEEF WITH PRUNES

1½ lb. lean stewing steak	1 pt. beer or guinness
Seasoned flour	Salt and freshly milled black
2 oz. dripping or white vegetable fat	pepper
	1 tbspn. tomato puree
2 medium onions peeled and finely chopped	8 prunes soaked for several hours
½ lb. new carrots	Chopped fresh parsley

Trim away any fat or gristle and cut the meat into neat pieces. Roll in seasoned flour. Heat the fat in a frying pan, add the meat and brown evenly on all sides. Lift the meat from the pan and place in casserole dish. Add the chopped onions and scraped, thinly chopped carrots to the casserole. Stir 1 tablespoon of the seasoned flour into the hot fat remaining in the frying pan.

If necessary add a littel extra fat to absorb the flour. Cook, stirring all the time, over moderate heat, until the mixture is well browned. Gradually stir in the beer and bring to the boil. Check seasoning with salt and pepper and stir in the tomato puree. Draw the pan off the heat and strain the gravy over the contents of the casserole dish. Cover the casserole dish with a tight fitting lid and place in the centre of a slow oven (300°f. or Gas No. 2) and cook for 2½ hours.

About 1 hour before the end of the cooking time add the drained prunes. If tenderised prunes are used add about 30 mins. before the end of the cooking time since they cook more quickly. Recover the casserole and continue to cook until meat, vegetables and prunes are tender. Sprinkle with chopped parsley and serve.

Serves 6   *Mrs. C. Moira, Stareton*

GUINEA FOWL STUFFED WITH OLIVES

1 Guinea Fowl   Fat streaky bacon

For the stuffing:

4 or 5oz. jar of olives stuffed
   with anchovies, or plain
   green olives

2 rounded tbspns. of
   chopped onion

3 oz. fresh breadcrumbs

1 oz. butter

1 small egg

For the sauce:

$\frac{1}{2}$ pt. of sour cream

Chop the olives. Fry the chopped onion gently in the butter until soft.

Mix them with the olives, the breadcrumbs and the egg, adding freshly ground black pepper but no salt. Stuff the guinea fowl with this mixture.

Cover it with the streaky bacon and cook in a moderate oven for 1-1$\frac{1}{2}$ hours.

For the sauce add the sour cream to the pan juices.

Serves 4 — 5   *Lady Beecham, Compton Scorpian*

(s) **PORK CHOPS BAKED IN CREAM**

4 thick pork chops

2 tbspns. butter

$\frac{1}{2}$ lb. finely chopped
   mushrooms

1 tbspn. lemon juice

1 tbspn. flour

Salt and black pepper

Thyme

4 tbspons. double cream

Finely chopped parsley

Trim excess fat from 4 good sized pork chops and saute in butter until golden on both sides. Remove from pan. Spoon off all but 2 tbspns. fat from pan and saute mushrooms until soft. Stir in lemon juice, sprinkle with flour and cook until slightly thickened and almost dry. Season with salt and pepper. Rub chops with little dried thyme and season to taste.

Cut 4 pieces of foil large enough to wrap each pork chop completely.

Brush foil with oil, place chop on one half, cover chops with mushroom mixture nd pour 1 tbspn. of cream over each chop. Sprinkle with parsley, fold foil over and seal edges well. Place on baking sheets and bake in a slow oven (325°f. — Mark 2) until chops are tender — 45-60 mins.

Serves 4   *Mrs. P. Wartnaby, Leek Wootton*

LOIN OF PORK

1 loin of pork (7-8 cutlets)	Sliced potatoes
4 tbspns. softened butter	18 glazed button onion
Crumbled thyme and bay leaf	18 sauteed mushroom caps
Salt and black pepper	Bouquet garni
2 tbspns olive oil	2 tbspns. finely chopped parsley

N.B. Ask butcher to remove the rind from the loin but retain the fat.

Mix softened butter, thyme and bay leaf to a smooth paste and rub into pork 3-4 hours before roasting. Sprinkle with salt and pepper and leave at room temperature.

Place pork fat side up in oven-proof casserole, add olive oil and roast in slow oven (350°f. — Mark 3) for about 1 hour and about half cooked. Peel and slice potatoes and place together with onions and mushrooms around pork.

Add a bouquet garni and continue cooking, basting often until tender.

Sprinkle with finely chopped parsley and serve.

Serves 6 — 8   *Mrs. P. Wartnaby, Leek Wootton*

(E)(S)   **TURKEY AND WALNUT PIE**

½ oz. butter
4 oz. mushrooms
½ oz. flour
¼ pt. double cream
2½ fl. oz. soured cream

Mixed herbs — sage, thyme,
   bay leaf
¾ lb. cooked turkey
2 oz. chopped walnuts

Fry sliced mushrooms for 3 mins. and remove from pan. Add flour to pan and mix with remaining fat. Add cream, soured cream, chopped herbs and bay leaf — boil, stirring all the time. Simmer 10 mins. Remove bay leaf. Season well.

Add turkey (cubed), walnuts and mushrooms. Pack in pie dish and cover with puff pastry. Bake at 450°f. until brown. 30 mins.

Serves 4 — 6   *Mrs. R. Bradley, Machynlleth, Wales*

COQ AU VIN

One 3½-4 lb. chicken
   jointed
2 tbspns. chopped garlic
1 medium onion sliced

1 carrot sliced
1 bottle red wine — cheap
Salt and pepper
12 peppercorns

Put a bottle of red wine in a pan with a sliced onion, carrot, peppercorns, giblets, salt and chopped garlic. Simmer for one hour. Fry chicken joints in olive oil, until golden and crispy. Sprinkle with a little flour and pour over the contents of wine pan. Simmer very slowly for about 2 hours until chicken is cooked through. Transfer chicken to serving dish and strain sauce over.

Use a cheap wine as the long simmering will remove the acidity and all the garlic becomes almost imperceptible.

Serves 4 — 6   *Mrs. J. M. Macnair, Ullenhall*

ROAST DUCKLING WITH WINE SAUCE

1 oven ready duckling (4$\frac{1}{2}$ 1 tbspn. hot water
  - 5lbs.)   Salt
2 tbspns. clear honey

Wine sauce:

$\frac{1}{4}$ pt. white wine $\frac{1}{2}$ oz. butter
$\frac{1}{4}$ pt. giblet stock   1 small onion finely chopped
Juice of half a lemon   1 oz. plain flour

Rub the skin of the duckling with salt and prick with prongs of a fork. Add two tbspns. cold water in roasting tin and place in centre of oven at 350°f. Cook 25 mins. per lb. After one hour of roasting time, pour away excess fat, blend honey and hot water and brush over the duckling. Return to the oven, repeating this once or twice until cooking time is complete. Pour away excess fat from the tin, leaving the dark dripping behind, to which add white wine, stock and lemon juice. Melt the butter in saucepan, gently fry the onion, add the flour, cook for a minute before adding the strained stock mixture. Carve the golden duckling, arrange on a dish and pour over the wine sauce.

Serves 3 — 4   *Mrs. J. Winstanley, Barford*

PIGEON PIE

2 pigeons
1 lb. rump steak
Dripping
1 onion
1 oz. flour
Salt and pepper

Bunch parsley and chopped
    parsley
2 rashers lean bacon
    (minced)
1 hard-boiled egg
Short pastry for a crust

Cut pigeons into small pieces and fry in dripping. Remove from pan and put aside to cool. Slice onion and fry in same dripping until lightly browned. Stir in the flour and when blended add ¾ pt. of water together with tied bunch of parsley and season with salt and pepper. Let the sauce simmer for 15 mins. Roll up small slices of the steak, dust with pepper and salt and place in the pie dish together with pigeon pieces. Sprinkle with chopped parsley and minced bacon and cover the dish with the prepared sauce. Cook in a moderate (325°) oven for one hour. Allow to cool then add slices of hard boiled egg and cover with pastry leaving a hole in the centre of crust. Brush with beaten egg and bake until nicely browned in a moderate oven.

Serves 4   *Mrs. S. Richardson, Nuneaton*

Ⓔ   **RICH HARE CASSEROLE**

1 hare
6 cloves of garlic
6 bay leaves
Peel of 1 lemon
¼ pt. olive oil
1 bottle cheap red wine

2 oz. seasoned flour
1 tspn. powdered cloves
2 oz. butter
1 tbspn. olive oil
Salt and pepper

Cut the meat off the hare bones and place in large dish. Roughly chop the garlic. Combine the bay leaves, lemon peel, olive oil and red wine to make a marinade. Adding the garlic, place over the meat and leave for at least 24 hours.

Drain meat following day and roll in the seasoned flour containing the cloves.

Melt butter and oil in flame-proof casserole and quickly brown meat and add remaining seasoned flour. Stir and allow to cook for a few minutes. Pour over the strained marinade and any wine left over. Bring to the boil and put in slow oven at 300°f. (Gas 2) for 5-6 hours. Serve with forcemeat balls, jacket potatoes and redcurrant jelly.

Make soup with all bones and remains of the hare.

Serves 4 — 6   *Mrs. P. Beney, Warwick*

☆ **BAKED BACON**

6 lb. forehock (boned and
   rolled)
½ bottle dry white wine
Bouquet garni
6 peppercorns
3 cloves

1 small onion
1 carrot
1 lb. can halved apricots
1 oz. butter
2 oz. white breadcrumbs
1 oz. blanched almonds

Bring bacon to boil in plain water. Drain. Place in pan with wine and fresh water to cover. Add bouquet garni, peppercorns, cloves, onion and carrot.

Bring to boil and simmer for 20 mins. to lb. and 20 mins. over. Drain joint and remove rind. Score fat diagonally. Bake at 400° (6) for 15 mins. to brown and crisp fat, basting occasionally with apricot juice. Keep fruit for salad. Melt butter in frying pan. Add breadcrumbs and coarsely chopped almonds, cook, stirring frequently until brown. Sprinkle hot crumbs over hot bacon fat. When cold decorate with pieces of apricot.

Serves 6 — 8   *Mrs. J. Snook, Kenilworth*

☆ VERY RICH CHOCOLATE MOUSSE

Mousse:

8 oz. semi-sweet chocolate	2 fl. oz. Grand Marnier
2 tbspns. castor sugar	³/₄ cup sponge cake crumbs
6 eggs separated	soaked together
8 oz. butter	

Glaze:

4 oz. semi-sweet chocolate	1 tbspn. water
2¹/₂ oz. butter	Flaked browned almonds
3 tbspns. Grand Marnier	

Mousse:

Melt chocolate in double boiler and add beaten egg yolks. Remove from heat and add butter gradually, beating until all the butter is incorporated.

Fold in Grand Marnier and soaked sponge cake. Fold in ¹/₃ of the stiffly beaten egg whites into the chocolate mixture. Then the remainder. Pour into buttered mould and refrigerate for at least 8 hours.

Glaze: (Make on day)

Melt chocolate in double boiler, add 3 tbspns. Grand Marnier and the water.

When combined remove from heat and add butter. Place over very low heat and stir until smooth and shiny. Allow to cool.

About 4 hours before serving, de-mould mousse and pour glaze over it.

Sprinkle with browned flaked almonds. Put back in 'fridge until serving time.

Serves 8   *Mrs. P. Breyfogle, Stareton*

JUBILEE MERINGUE or
GINGER MERINGUE

3 egg whites ⎫
6 oz. sugar ⎬ for meringue
1 tbspn. ginger syrup ⎭

6 pieces stem ginger
1 small tin pineapple pieces
$\frac{1}{2}$ pt. double cream

Make meringue. Divide mixture in half and place on two baking sheets in rounds. Cook. Whip cream and add ginger syrup. Spread the whipped cream on one meringue round, and then slice ginger and pineapple pieces and place on top of the cream. Then place other meringue round on the top.

Serves 8 — 10   *Mrs. J. Scroggs, Warwick*

Ⓢ   # CHOCOLATE GATEAU

Base:
6 oz. digestive biscuits   2-3 oz. butter

Top:
2 oz. butter
6 oz. sugar
2 oz. chocolate (Bournville)

1 tspn. vanilla essence
3 eggs

Make a biscuit base melting the butter and adding the crushed biscuits.

Place firmly into a greased dish. Cream butter and sugar well. Add the melted chocolate and vanilla essence. Beat in the eggs, one at a time and pour mixture on top of the biscuit base. Leave in the 'fridge for approximately 4 hours — delicious!

Serves 6 — 8   *Miss J. Gladstone, Benson*

131

☆ **WINTER PUDDING from Crete**

8 oz. dried figs
4 oz. raisins
8 oz. dates
3 oz. ginger (in a piece)
2-3 tbspns. cheap brandy
6 oz. breadcrumbs
8 oz. self-raising flour

6 oz. suet (chopped well)
Pinch of salt
3 eggs
Rind (grated) and juice of 1 lemon
Little milk

Slice and chop the figs, raisins, dates and ginger. Put into a small bowl and add the brandy. Cover carefully and leave to stand for at least one hour.

Mix together the crumbs, suet, flour and salt. Add to the well beaten eggs with the lemon juice, rind and finally the fruit mixture. Mix together and add the milk if the consistency is too thick.

Grease a pudding basin. Put the mixture into the basin. Cover carefully and steam for 4 hours or so — the longer the better.

Turn out and serve with: whipped cream, or maple syrup, ice-cream or Christmas pudding sauce (for a special party) or hot custard sauce (for a family meal).

Very warming, satisfying and rich. Needs a good walk afterwards, but well worth the calorie count.

Serves 8 — 10 *Mrs. J. Butterworth, Coventry*

Ⓢ☆Ⓕ RICH CHOCOLATE PUDDING

6 oz. bitter chocolate	³/₄ pt. cream
1 oz. butter	1 oz. sugar
6 egg yolks	Grated chocolate
6 egg whites	

Melt chocolate and butter over gentle heat. Add yolks. Whip whites and fold into chocolate. Whip cream with sugar until thick and line a pudding basin. Put in freezer to harden. Add chocolate and put back in refrigerator. Unmould two hours before serving. Turn onto dish and put back in 'fridge. Cover with grated chocolate.

Serves 6 — 8   *The Lady Cranworth, Suffolk*

Ⓔ Ⓢ   MOCCA LOG

3 oz. butter	1 pt. strong black coffee
2¹/₂ oz. castor sugar	(4 tbspns. Nescafe to 1 pt.
2 egg yolks	boiling water)
2 packets "Nice" biscuits	1 oz. grated plain chocolate

Dip the biscuits into the coffee 2 at a time until soaked but not broken.

Place a layer of 6 on a plate. Beat together the yolks, sugar and butter until creamy enough to spread. Spread a little over the biscuits then add another layer of soaked biscuits followed by a layer of the filling. Alternate until all is used and leave to cool. Cover with grated plain chocolate. Serve in slices not more than 1″ thick.

Serves 6 — 8   *Mrs. K. Mansell, Herefordshire*

CHOCOLATE ROULADE

6 oz. block chocolate   5 eggs
8 oz. castor sugar   3-4 tbspns. water

½ pt. double cream whipped and flavoured with vanilla, rum or brandy and icing sugar. Shallow swiss roll tin 12″ x 8″.

Line tin with oiled paper. Set oven 350°. Separate eggs, add yolks slowly to sugar beating till mixture is lemon coloured. Melt chocolate in water in pan over gentle heat, when like thick cream draw pan off.

Whip whites to firm snow then add chocolate to egg yolk mixture; cut and fold egg whites into mixture and turn into prepared tin. Place in pre-set oven and bake 10-15 mins. or until firm to the touch. Have ready a clean cloth wrung out in cold water. Take out roulade, cool slightly then cover with the cloth (to prevent crust forming). Leave in a cool place or 'fridge over night. Lay a piece of greaseproof paper on table, dust well with icing sugar. Remove cloth and turn roulade upside down on prepared paper, strip paper case off carefully. Good cut in three and tiered with cream and saves all fuss of rolling.

Serves 8   *Mrs. T. Royle, Ilmington*

E S   **LEMON OR ORANGE FLUFF**

Rind and juice of 2 lemons   3-4oz. sugar
    made up to ½ pt. with water   2 eggs
1 tbsp. cornflour

Blend cornflour with a little water and bring lemons and juice and water to boil. Add to cornflour and cook until thickened. Add sugar and egg yolks, cook gently for a few minutes and put on one side to become cold. Beat egg whites until stiff, fold into mixture and put into glass dishes.

This is very light and refreshing after a rich meal.

Serve 4 — 6   *Mrs. P. Beney, Warwick*

Ⓢ   DEEP FREEZE BRANDY CAKE

$\frac{1}{2}$ lb. Digestive biscuits   2 eggs
$\frac{1}{2}$ lb. bitter chocolate   3 oz. sugar
$\frac{1}{2}$ lb. butter   Wineglass of Brandy

Crush biscuits not too small. Melt chocolate and butter over gentle heat.

Beat eggs and sugar until creamy. Mix into melted chocolate and butter.

Fold in biscuits and wineglass of brandy. Pour into mould an place in freezer taking out $\frac{1}{2}$ hour before serving. Keeps well in freezer.

Walnuts and glace cherries can be added if liked.

Serves 6 — 10   *The Lady Cranworth, Suffolk*

PINEAPPLE PUDDING

4 oz. butter   Tin pineapple pieces
Butter puffs   4 oz. carton double cream
2 eggs
1 cup icing sugar

Cream icing sugar and butter, add 2 whole eggs and beat. Crush butter puffs and add about $\frac{1}{2}$ packet to mixture. Put mixture in bottom of dish. Beat cream, fold in 1 tbspn. icing sugar, then fold in drained pineapple pieces.

Put on top of mixture, decorate with some crushed butter puffs and pineapple.

Serves 6   *Mrs. T. Royle, Ilmington*

[E] [S]

LEMON DELIGHT

2 pt. oven dish
2 oz. margarine
4 oz. castor sugar
1 oz. plain flour

1 lemon, juice and rind
½ pt. milk
2 eggs, separated

Cream fat and sugar, stir in flour, juice, rind and yolks. Blend in milk. Fold in stiffly beaten egg whites. Place dish in bain marie in moderate oven (325° or Mark 4) for ¾ hour-1 hour.

Serves 4
Mrs. Dickinson, Warwick

[E]

LEMON MOUSSE WITH CHOCOLATE AND ALMONDS

3-4 lemons approx. 8 oz. lemon juice
2 tspns. grated rind
½ oz. packet of gelatine
4 tbspns. cold water

4 eggs
7 oz. castor sugar
2 tbspns. almost boiling water

Squeeze lemons and grate rind. Measure cold water in saucepan and sprinkle in the gelatine. Leave to soak. Separate the egg yolks from the whites.

Add 6 oz. of the sugar to the yolks and start to whip adding the almost boiling water. Whip until very thick and light. Meanwhile dissolve the gelatine over gentle heat, and pour into the lemon juice. If using a mixer, pour through the sieve gradually into the whipped mixture whilst still whipping. Add lemon rind. Place in freezer until nearly set. Only then whip the egg whites until stiff and add the remaining ounce of sugar, whipping for a further minute. Fold this into the lemon mixture and pour into a glass dish or individual glasses. When set, decorate with grated chocolate and finely chopped almonds.

Serves 6 — 8
Mrs. J. Winstanley, Barford

Ⓕ ✪   **CHRISTMAS ICE PUDDING**

6 oz. of a combination of any of the following:-
Glace cherries, glace orange, raisins, currants, marrons glace
4 tbspns. rum
½ pt. single cream

5 egg yolks
5 oz. castor sugar
4 oz. unsweetened chestnut puree
4 oz. bitter chocolate
½ pt. double cream

Chop the dried and glace fruits roughly and soak in rum. Heat the single cream almost to boiling point, mix egg yolks and sugar and pour warm cream over and return to pan. Stir over gentle heat in double saucepan until mixture thickens — (but do not boil). When thickened add chestnut puree and chocolate and stir well until they have dissolved and custard is quite smooth.

Test for sweetness and leave to cool. Mix in the fruits and finally fold in the whipped double cream.

Ideal for freezing. To serve — remove from deep freeze 1 hr. before serving and place in 'fridge.

Not suitable for younger members of the family — very rich — most delicious.

Serves 6 — 8   *Mrs. P. Wartnaby, Leek Wootton*

(E)(S)   ## WINTER HEALTH SALAD

Grate equal amounts of raw fennel, carrot, celery and white cabbage.

Add a few finely chopped walnuts. Make a French dressing adding lemon juice and a little caster sugar. Toss all ingredients together and sprinkle with freshly ground black pepper. Very economical, as only small amount of each are required.

Mrs. J. Winstanley, Barford

(E)(S) ## CARROTS WITH GARLIC BUTTER

Thick Julienne strips carrot cooked until tender in boiling salted water.

Drian and toss in prepared garlic butter. Dust with chopped parsley.

Garlic butter:

1 clove garlic crushed in salt   2 oz. butter   Black pepper

Mrs. P. Beney, Warwick

(E)(S)   ## CABBAGE ALSASCIENNE

1 hard white cabbage   1 wine glass dry cider, dry
1 large onion   sherry or white wine
2 oz. butter   Salt and black pepper

Slice onion on Mandolin slicer, very thinly. Soften in butter until transparent.

Julienne strips of celery can be added at this stage for a change.

Slice cabbage. Add to pan, pour cider over. Season well. Put on lid and cook for 5 mins., shaking pan well.

Serves 4   *Mrs. P. Beney, Warwick*

RED CABBAGE

1 medium sized red cabbage	10 peppercorns
2 or 3 onions	Salt
2 or 3 apples quartered	3 or 4 tbspns. vinegar
2 or 3 oz. sultanas	3 or 4 oz. lard or cooking oil
6 cloves	

Shred cabbage finely. Slice onions. Toss cabbage and onions in melted lard or oil in large shallow pan which should have a close fitting lid. Add the apples, sultanas, seasonings and vinegar. Stir and thoroughly mix. Then cover and cook gently for 2 or 3 hours on very low heat or in a very slow oven, stirring occasionally. If the mixture is not fluid enough, add a little hot water.

Serves 6 — 8   *Lady Beecham, Compton Scorpian*

Ⓔ Ⓢ Ⓕ   ## FLAPJACKS

9 oz. soft margarine	12 oz. "porridge" oats
9 oz. soft brown sugar	2 oz. sultanas

Mix together margarine and sugar in large bowl. Add oats, stir in. Fold in sultanas.

Place in 2 x 7″ square greased tins and pat level.

Bake at 350°f./Gas 4 for 20-25 mins., until just coloured.

Remove from oven. Allow to cool a little, and mark into squares with the back of a knife. When cold break into squares along markings.

Store in airtight tin.

(Can also be frozen — as for ordinary biscuits and cakes).

Children's tea-time standby. Also good for cricket teas!

Mrs. M. Rushton, Leaminton Spa

TARTLETTES au GINGEMBRE

3 oz. butter
3 oz. plain flour
Juice ½ lemon

3 oz. golden syrup
1 tspn. ground ginger
3 oz. sugar

Filling:

½ pt. double cream
1 egg white

6-7 pieces stem ginger
1 tbspn. brandy

Sift flour and ginger together and put to warm on a plate. Melt butter, sugar and treacle together, do not over-heat. Stir in flour and lemon juice and mix well. Place in teaspoonful on a buttered baking sheet, allowing room to spread, cook for 7-10 mins. at 300°f. or Reg. 2-3.

Remove carefully and cool over the base of inverted 1 lb jam jars (oil jars lightly for first batch tarts.) Place on a rack when crisp.

These store for 2-3 days in a tin.

Filling:

Whip the cream firmly, chop most of the ginger and stir into cream together with the brandy. Whip egg white stiffly and fold into cream. Fill each tartlet with some mixture and decorate with the rest of the ginger sliced.

N.B. The tartlets must not be filled until shortly before needed, as they go soft very quickly.

Other fillings such as mandarin or black cherries in season can also be used.

Mrs. J. Cozens, Horley

E S F

GREEN HERB AND LEMON STUFFING

(Turkey stuffing)

7 oz. fresh white breadcrumbs	Pepper
3 oz. suet	2 small eggs
Finely grated rind of 1 lemon	3-4 tbspns. milk
1½ level tspns. salt	4 level tspns. parsley
	Juice of 1 lemon

Mix crumbs, suet, lemon rind and juice and seasoning together with parsley.

Beat eggs and milk together. Bind into mixture, but do not overwork.

Fill into turkey.

Mrs. P. Wartnaby, Leek Wootton

GRATIN DAUPHINOIS

2 lbs. potatoes	4 oz. grated Emmenthal cheese
Salt and pepper to taste	Garlic to taste
¼ pint hot milk	¼ pint, single cream
2 oz. Butter in cubes	

Cut potatoes in very thin slices. Layer in dish with butter, seasoning and crushed garlic. Add hot milk. Cover dish and cook in middle of hot oven for ¾ hour.

Add cream and sprinkle with cheese.

Place under grill and brown well.

Serve very hot.

Serves 4　　　　　　　　　*Mademoiselle P. Froget, France*

(E) (S) (F)   ## GINGERBREAD

12 oz. S.R. flour
4 oz. dark sugar
4 oz. fat
1 cup of black treacle
⅔ cup of boiling water

2 eggs
1½ tspns. ground ginger
½ tspn. mixed spice
1 tspn. bicarbonate of soda

Sift flour and spice in large bowl.
  Melt fat, sugar and treacle in pan.
  Make a well and stir in melted ingredients to make batter.
  Add beaten eggs and 1 tbspn. milk.
  Add boiling water to consistency of double cream.
  Stir in bicarb dissolved in 1 tbspn. water.
  Pour into greased tin.
  Bake ¾ hour - 1 hour in moderate oven.

Mrs. Dickinson, Warwick

(E) (F)   ## LEEK TART

6 medium leeks
1½ oz. butter
2 whole eggs and one yolk
½ pt. creamy milk

Salt and pepper
Nutmeg
1 oz. grated Parmesan
6 oz. shortcrust pastry

Bake an 8 inch flan case.
  Clean the leeks, cutting away the darker green of the leaves, and slice them finely. Soften them in butter, seasoning them with salt, pepper and nutmeg. Pre-heat the oven to Reg. 4 (350°f.). Beat the eggs and milk, stir in the leeks and cheese. You can add some streaky bacon cut into sticks and blanched in boiling water for 5 mins.
  Pour the mixture in to the flan case and bake for 30 mins. until the flan is set, firm but still creamy.

Serves 6   *Mrs. P. Scroggs, Warwick*

AMERICAN LEMON BARS

¹/₂ lb. plain sifted flour   ¹/₂ lb. butter   4 oz. icing sugar

Mix like pastry and press into pan (10″ x 15″) and bake 355°
for about 15 mins.

Mix:

4 beaten eggs   4 tbspns. plain flour
1 lb. sugar   1 tspn. baking powder
Rind and juice of 2 lemons

Pour over crust and bake in pre-set oven 350°f. about 20 mins.
or a little longer. Let stand and sprinkle powdered sugar on top,
loosen custard round edge with a knife. Cut into bars.

Mrs. T. Royle, Ilmington

(E)(S)   **GARLIC STUFFED ONIONS**

6 Spanish onions   6 tbspns. finely chopped
12 large cloves garlic   parsley
Olive oil   Fresh breadcrumbs
Salt and black pepper   Butter

Simmer onions and garlic in boiling salted water until tender.
Scoop out centre of onions. Combine flesh of onions with
cooked garlic, finely chop. then pound together until smooth
with olive oil, salt and black pepper, chopped parsley and 6
tbspns. of fresh breadcrumbs. Stuff onions with this mixture,
place on greased baking dish and sprinkle with further
breadcrumbs, dot with butter until cooked through.

   Delicious with lamb chops!

Serves 6   *Mrs. P. Wartnaby, Leek Wootton*

Ⓔ Ⓢ Ⓕ   **ONION MEAT BALLS**

2 medium onions
1 lb. minced beef
1 lb. sausage meat (pork)
4 oz. packet sage and onion
    stuffing mix
1 egg, lighly beaten
$\frac{1}{2}$ tspn. salt
$\frac{1}{4}$ tspn. black pepper

One 10$\frac{1}{2}$ oz. can condensed
    Oxtail soup (Campbells)
$\frac{1}{2}$ pt. water
1 green pepper, de-seeded
    and cut in rings
1 red pepper, de-seeded and
    cut in rings
6 oz. mushrooms, sliced

Grate onions into large bowl. Add meats and stuffing mix. Add egg and seasoning, stir well to mix.

Form into small balls (about 48). Place closely together in casserole. Mix soup and water, add peppers and mushrooms and pour over.

Bake (350°f./Gas 4) for 1 hour.

To serve now: Serve hot with rice, spaghetti or fried potatoes and green salad.

To freeze: Transfer meat balls on slotted spoon to rigid container, pour over sauce. Seal. Label. Use within 3 months.

To serve from freezer, thaw over night in 'fridge or 4 hours at room temperature.

Heat in casserole (325°f./Gas 3) for 30 mins. Serve hot.

Serves 12   *Mrs. M. Rushton, Leamington Spa*

⑤ **OLDE WORLDE MINCEMEAT**

1½ lbs. cooking apples
1½ lbs. stoned raisins
¾ lb. currants
6 oz. butter
¾ lb. soft brown sugar
2 level dspns. ground cinnamon

4 tbspns. brandy or rum
2 level tspns. each —
ground cloves, nutmeg mace
¼ pt. cider
4 tbspns. golden syrup
Grated rind and juice of 2 lemons

Cut apples in quarters, remove, core, chop coarsely and mix with raisins, currants, butter and sugar and spices.

Bring the cider to the boil, stir in fruit, butter, sugar and spices together with syrup and juice of lemons.

Takes about ½ hour to come to the boil. Cover and simmer gently for 30-40 mins. stirring occasionally. Cool for a few minutes.

Stir in brandy or rum, then pack in clean warm jars. Cover and label.

Makes approx. 6 lbs   *Mrs. P. Wartnaby, Leek Wootton*

CONVERSION TABLES

OVEN TEMPERATURES

	Degrees Farenheit	Regulo	Degrees Centigrade
Very slow	200-280	$\frac{1}{4}$ - $\frac{1}{2}$	115 - 135
Slow	280 - 320	1	135 - 160
Warm	320 - 340	3	160 - 170
Moderate	340 - 370	4	170 - 185
Fairly hot	370 - 400	5 - 6	185 - 205
Hot	400 - 440	7	205 - 225
Very hot	440 - 500	8 - 9	225 - 250

METRIC WEIGHTS

1 kilogramme	= 2.2046 lb. = 2 lb. $3\frac{1}{4}$ oz.
7 grammes	= $\frac{1}{4}$ oz.
14 grammes	= $\frac{1}{2}$ oz.
21 grammes	= $\frac{3}{4}$ oz.
28 grammes	= 1 oz.
$453\frac{1}{2}$ grammes	= 1 lb.

FLUIDS

1 litre	= 35 fluid oz. = $1\frac{3}{4}$ pints (almost exactly)
$\frac{1}{2}$ litre	= $17\frac{1}{2}$ fluid oz.
1 litre	= 1000 cc (or ml - millimetres)

ENGLISH MEASURES

1 pint	= 20 fluid oz.	= 568 cc
1 gill	= 5 fluid oz. ($\frac{1}{4}$ pint)	= 142 cc
Bottle Table wine	= 24 fluid oz.	= 680 cc
1 pound (lb)	= 16 oz.	

146

AMERICAN MEASURES

1 pint	= 16 fluid oz.	= 453 cc
1 cup	= 8 fluid oz.	= 227 cc
½ cup	= 4 tablespoonsful of fluid	
1 cup butter	= 5 oz.	= 142 gms
1 cup grated cheese	= 3½ oz.	= 98 gms
1 cup sugar	= 7½ oz.	= 223 gms
1 cup flour	= 4½ oz.	= 128 gms

GELATINE

1oz. gelatine will stiffen 1 pint fluid or fruit juice
½ oz. gelatine will stiffen 1 pint mayonnaise or thick sauce

GLOSSARY

bain-marie — culinary water bath. A large open vessel, half filled with hot water in which saucepans containing sauces, etc., are placed so that their contents are kept nearly at boiling point without burning or reducing.

gall — core, ducts, tubes etc., that occur in liver and kidneys.

julienne strips — very long thinly sliced strips

macerate — to crush or soften by steeping in a liquid

marinade — a mixture of oil, herbs, vinegar etc., in which fish or meat is soused or pickled

pare — to peel thinly without pith

ramekin — a small fire proof mould for serving individual savoury dishes

sauté — food cooked, or tossed in fat without being browned: this can be done by covering food with buttered paper during cooking

zest — the juice from the coloure doily outer skin of citrus fruits

Index

INDEX

148

Index

Index